Energy and Material Resources

Attitudes, Values, and Public Policy

AAAS Selected Symposia Series

Published by Westview Press, Inc.
5500 Central Avenue, Boulder, Colorado

for the

American Association for the Advancement of Science
1776 Massachusetts Ave., N.W., Washington, D.C.

Energy and Material Resources

Attitudes, Values, and Public Policy

Edited by W. David Conn

Routledge
Taylor & Francis Group
LONDON AND NEW YORK

First published 1983 by Westview Press

Published 2018 by Routledge
52 Vanderbilt Avenue, New York, NY 10017
2 Park Square, Milton Park, Abingdon, Oxon OX14 4RN

Routledge is an imprint of the Taylor & Francis Group, an informa business

Library of Congress Catalog Card Number 82-62058

ISBN 13: 978-0-367-01966-2(hbk)

ISBN 13: 978-0-367-16953-4(pbk)

About the Book

Knowledge of public attitudes and values is essential to the formulation and implementation of government policies affecting energy and other natural resources, but it is difficult to obtain and use this knowledge, for the pertinent issues are complex and involve such difficult-to-define concepts as degree of acceptable risk for both present and future generations. Recently, survey researchers have attempted to measure and explain public attitudes related to energy and resource conservation. This volume examines what policymakers need to or would like to know about these attitudes, what kinds of results the researchers have been able to obtain, and the extent to which their results currently influence the policymaking process.

About the Series

The *AAAS Selected Symposia Series* was begun in 1977 to provide a means for more permanently recording and more widely disseminating some of the valuable material which is discussed at the AAAS Annual National Meetings. The volumes in this *Series* are based on symposia held at the Meetings which address topics of current and continuing significance, both within and among the sciences, and in the areas in which science and technology impact on public policy. The *Series* format is designed to provide for rapid dissemination of information, so the papers are not typeset but are reproduced directly from the camera-copy submitted by the authors. The papers are organized and edited by the symposium arrangers who then become the editors of the various volumes. Most papers published in this *Series* are original contributions which have not been previously published, although in some cases additional papers from other sources have been added by an editor to provide a more comprehensive view of a particular topic. Symposia may be reports of new research or reviews of established work, particularly work of an interdisciplinary nature, since the AAAS Annual Meetings typically embrace the full range of the sciences and their societal implications.

WILLIAM D. CAREY
Executive Officer
American Association for the Advancement of Science

Contents

About the Editor and Authors

W. David Conn, *an environmental planner, is associate professor and chair of the doctoral program in the College of Architecture and Urban Studies, Virginia Polytechnic Institute and State University, Blacksburg. He is the author of numerous articles and reports on resource conservation, solid waste management, and air quality planning.*

Frederick W. Allen *is chief of the Energy Development Branch of the Environmental Protection Agency. In 1978-79 he served as staff director for the Resource Conservation Committee, a Cabinet-level interagency committee formed to study policies affecting the use and conservation of material resources. He is coauthor of the committee's report,* **Choices for Conservation** *(GPO, 1979).*

Lynda T. Carlson, *chief of the Residential and Commercial Branch of the Energy End Use Division at the Department of Energy, has specialized in energy consumption and survey design methodology. While at DOE she has been involved in major surveys to determine energy consumption patterns for residential and nonresidential areas.*

Riley E. Dunlap *is associate professor of sociology and rural sociology at Washington State University, Pullman. A specialist in environmental sociology, he has published more than two dozen articles in his field, particularly on public attitudes toward environmental issues.*

Barbara Farhar-Pilgrim, *a consulting sociologist, was a senior social scientist at the Solar Energy Research Institute in Golden, Colorado, where she initiated the National Study of the Residential Solar Consumer to explore the attitudes, knowledge, and practices of consumers with regard to energy conservation and solar technologies. Her book,* **America's Solar Potential: A National Consumer Study** *(written with C. Unseld; Praeger, 1982), presents the results of this study.*

A specialist in interactions between technology and society, she has done research on decision processes, the social aspects of energy and solar energy, social impacts assessments, weather modification, and the diffusion of innovations.

Baruch Fischhoff *is research associate at Decision Research (a branch of Perceptronics, Inc.) in Eugene, Oregon; visiting associate professor of psychology at the University of Oregon at Eugene; and visiting scientist at the Medical Research Council/Applied Psychology Unit in Cambridge, England. A specialist in risk perception, judgment, and decision-making, he is the author of numerous books and articles in his field, most recently* **Acceptable Risk** *(with S. Lichtenstein et al.; Cambridge University Press, 1981).*

J. Keith Grieneeks, *a clinical psychologist at the Southlake Center for Mental Health in Lowell, Indiana, has done research on values and attitudes, energy consumption patterns of the Pacific Northwest, rural community development, and recreational use of wilderness land.*

Sarah Lichtenstein *is a research associate at Decision Research (a branch of Perceptronics, Inc.) in Eugene, Oregon, and adjunct professor of psychology at the University of Oregon, Eugene. Her research interests are judgment and decision-making, decision aids, and risk assessment. She is a coauthor of* **Acceptable Risk** *(with B. Fischhoff et al.; Cambridge University Press, 1981).*

Barbara Desow Melber, *a research scientist at the Social Change Study Center at Battelle Memorial Institute in Seattle, Washington, has specialized in public opinion and public participation related to energy policy. She is coauthor of* **Nuclear Power and the Public** *(with S. M. Nealey et al.; Lexington, forthcoming).*

Jon D. Miller *is associate dean for research at Northern Illinois University. His research interests include public attitudes, political behavior, and quantitative methods, and he is coauthor of* **Citizenship in an Age of Science** *(with R. W. Suchner and A. M. Voelker) and* **The American People and Science Policy** *(with K. Prewitt; Pergamon, 1980 and 1982, respectively).*

Harry J. Otway, *head of the Technology Assessment Sector at the Commission of the European Communities Joint Research Centre in Ispra, Italy, has published extensively on various aspects of risk analysis, attitude measurement, human performance, and policy analysis. He has been visiting professor of psychology and of engineering at the University of Illinois* *at Champaign and visiting scholar at the Social Science Research Institute at the University of Southern California. He is coauthor of* **Human and Organizational Aspects of New Office Technology** *(with M. Peltu; London: Francis Pinter, forthcoming).*

William L. Rankin, *a research scientist in the Social Change Study Center at Battelle Memorial Institute in Seattle, Washington, has been studying public attitudes toward energy technologies for more than six years. He has published on value measurement techniques, behavior change following value change, attitudes toward nuclear power and nuclear waste management, and media coverage of energy technologies. In 1978 he received the American Nuclear Society's Best Paper Award.*

Milton Rokeach *is professor of sociology and psychology at Washington State University at Pullman. A former fellow at the Center for Advanced Study in the Behavioral Sciences, he is the author of numerous books and articles, including* **Beliefs, Attitudes, and Values** *(Jossey-Bass, 1968) and* **The Nature of Human Values** *and* **Understanding Human Values** *(Free Press, 1973 and 1979, respectively).*

Paul Slovic *is a research associate at Decision Research (a branch of Perceptronics, Inc.) in Eugene, Oregon, and adjunct professor of psychology at the University of Oregon, Eugene. His specialties include judgment, decision-making, and risk assessment, and he has written or edited numerous publications on these topics, most recently* **Judgment Under Uncertainty: Heuristics and Biases** *(edited with D. Kahneman; Cambridge University Press, 1982). He is president-elect of the Society for Risk Analysis, a fellow of the American Psychological Association, and a member of the editorial boards of several professional journals.*

Seymour Warkov *is professor of sociology and associate director of the Center for the Study of Public Policy at the University of Connecticut. His specialties are social organization, energy and society, and evaluation research. His publications include* **Energy Policy in the United States: Social and Behavioral Dimensions** *(Praeger, 1978) and* **Solar Diffusion and Public Incentives** *(with J. W. Meyer; Lexington, 1982).*

W. David Conn

1. Introduction and Overview

Many attitudinal surveys conducted in the past decade or so have included questions on topics relating to the production and use of material and, especially, energy resources. In presenting the results of these surveys, the researchers have often suggested or asserted that they hold significance for public policymaking, and indeed one might expect this to be so. However, since most policymakers are not themselves experts in attitudinal research, it cannot be taken for granted that they can or will make proper use of the data. On the one hand, for example, the researchers may not be measuring what the policymakers really want to know, or they may not be asking the right people. On the other hand, the policymakers may not possess a sufficient understanding of the strengths and weaknesses of the whole approach to permit an appropriate interpretation of the results.

As an economist/planner with a major interest in materials policy (but without specific expertise in attitudinal research) I have found that the links between researchers and policymakers have not always been drawn very tightly. This volume sets out to bridge the gap by presenting a selection of papers that consider what policymakers in the materials and energy fields might be interested in knowing, what kinds of results the researchers are able to obtain, and the extent to which the results are actually used in the policymaking process.

In this introductory chapter I first draw attention to the fact that terms such as "attitudes," "beliefs," and "values" are used differently by different people; next, I briefly review the kinds of information that are likely to be of interest to policymakers concerned with material and energy resources (with illustrations from the materials field); then,

I identify some special problems faced by policymakers in these particular fields; and finally, I present an overview of the chapters to follow.

Use of Terms

Potentially a source of great confusion for non-experts in attitudinal research is the fact that different people use terms such as "attitudes," "beliefs," and "values" in different ways. While it might not necessarily be desirable or possible to force a consensus on the way that terms are used, it seems important to achieve mutual understanding on the use of a term in a specific instance. In this section I draw attention to some differences commonly encountered. The authors of later chapters in this volume were asked to clarify their own terminologies.

One of the simplest statements that distinguishes between attitudes, beliefs, and behavior has been made by Dillman (1978); he describes them as follows:

> Attitudes - what people say they want;
> Beliefs - what people think is true;
> Behavior - what people do.

Although his description of "behavior" seems to be fairly generally accepted, his distinction between the other two terms is not universally shared. Dillman expands on his simple statement by adding that attitudes describe how people feel about something; they are evaluative in nature and reflect respondents' views about the desirability of something." On the other hand, he argues, "beliefs are assessments of what a person thinks is true or false. There is no implied goodness or badness in beliefs, but only an assessment of what one thinks exists or does not exist." Another way of making this distinction is to say that attitudes are *normative*; that is, they are not subject to empirical verification since they are ultimately based on values. In contrast, beliefs are *positive*; that is, they are subject (at least in principle) to empirical testing, and can be shown to be correct or incorrect.

Among other authors, however, Rokeach (1973) makes different use of the terminology. He defines belief as "any simple proposition ... capable of being preceded by the phrase *I believe that* ...." Such a proposition may be evaluative; indeed, Rokeach specifically identifies "existential beliefs" which are of the true-false kind, and "evaluative beliefs" which are of the "good-bad" type. Rokeach reserves the term "attitude" for a "relatively enduring organization of inter-related beliefs that describe, evaluate, and advocate action with respect to an object or situation." The normative-positive distinction between beliefs and attitudes no longer holds in Rokeach's terminology. It is clear that these differences are significant, and should be understood by anyone wishing to use the results of attitudinal research.

Another term that is often used with different meanings is "value." Economists, for example, typically talk about values that objects or situations have for people, and examine preferences revealed in the marketplace as indicators of these values. Attitudes may also be expressions of these values, although economists are generally cautious in their interpretation of attitudinal data; they usually point to observed discrepancies between what people say and what they do, and argue that the only way to find out what people truly feel and want is to observe their behavior when faced with "real" choices.

However, the term "value" itself may be used differently. For example, Rokeach (1968) defines "human value" as "a single belief that transcendently guides actions and judgments across specific objects and situations and beyond immediate goals to more ultimate end states of existence" (note that "belief" here is used in the evaluative sense). Another explanation is given by McAllister (1980), who suggests that "human values serve as guides for personal decision-making, attaching significance and importance to objects and events, directing choices toward things considered desirable or good and away from things considered undesirable or bad. Seldom is only a single value involved in a decision; most require selecting and weighing several values simultaneously."

Once again, it seems important not so much to force the use of a single definition, but rather to ensure that differences in terminology, when they arise, are clearly recognized and understood.

Information that Policymakers Might Like to Have

To the non-expert, attitudinal research appears to have the potential of providing a great deal of useful information to policymakers concerned with material and energy resources. Later contributions to this volume are intended to explore whether this potential is or can be realized. In this section I briefly review some of the kinds of information that policymakers might like to have, giving illustrations from the materials field.

Beliefs

People's beliefs about past, present, and future states of affairs are likely to be of interest. What, for example, are their beliefs about the causes of past materials shortages? ... about our present dependence on foreign suppliers? ... about current rates of recycling? ... about the likelihood of materials scarcities in the future? ... about our per-capita use of materials in relation to per-capita uses elsewhere in the world? If some of these beliefs are known to be erroneous, policymakers may wish to give attention to correcting them; in the meantime, however, they are likely to be especially cautious in interpreting other survey responses that may themselves be influenced by mis-information.

Behavior

Policymakers may be expected to have an interest in reported behavior, at least to the extent that it can be assumed to approximate actual behavior. Do people use throw-away items such as plates and cutlery? ... do they separate and recycle their newspapers? ... have they installed flow restrictors on shower heads? In alerting policymakers as to how people are acting under present conditions, such information may be used, for example, to assess the effectiveness of policy measures taken in the past, as well as to provide a baseline from which to gauge the effectiveness of policy measures newly introduced.

Attitudes

Beliefs and reported behavior are *positive* items of information (in the sense discussed earlier); if we turn now to the *normative* information that might be obtained from surveys, we find that policymakers are likely to be interested in people's preferences regarding both the different goals and objectives (i.e. the *ends*) which might be adopted for public policy, and the *means* for achieving them.

Examples of ends-related questions are: what might the government attempt to achieve with a materials policy, if it should have one at all? ... how should trade-offs with other, competing social priorities be resolved? ... what level of accessibility to materials is considered equitable for those living in poorer countries, and for future generations? Means-related questions include: to what extent should emphasis be placed on conservation measures rather than measures to increase supply? ... if shortages occur, should there be rationing by allocation? ... by price? ... should the government attempt to control or influence the way products are packaged, and if so, how?

To the extent that attitudes are thought to reflect what people truly want, policymakers might be expected to seek attitudinal data on questions of this kind, both in order to guide the initial selection of policies and programs and to aid in anticipating the subsequent level of public support for those chosen.

Inter-Relationships

Policymakers are likely to be interested not only in acquiring information regarding individual attributes (i.e., beliefs, behavior, attitudes) but also in exploring the interrelationships between these attributes and the ways in which they relate to underlying human values (as defined by Rokeach). One purpose is for policymakers to obtain some understanding of why people think and act in the ways they do and, perhaps, of how they might be influenced to act differently; another purpose is to develop models that can be used to predict how the attributes might change in the future.

Special Problems

As will become evident later in this volume, supplying policymakers with the kinds of information discussed in the previous section can prove a difficult task. In the materials and energy fields, particularly, there are some special problems, as illustrated by the following:

1. Policymakers in these fields must deal with technical complexities that neither the public at large nor, in many cases, even the technical experts fully understand. For example, many people do not appreciate the crucial distinction between a "reserve" and a "resource" and therefore risk being misled by forecasts of future materials availability based solely on estimates of reserves. The fact that the intricacies of the tax system, and its impact on the use of virgin rather than recycled materials, challenge the understanding even of professional researchers, provides another illustration. Under these circumstances, the results of attitudinal surveys must be treated with special caution.

2. Another problem is that policymakers must make many decisions today in anticipation of future events that cannot be predicted with any certainty. It is difficult or impossible, for example, to predict the size and location of new mineral discoveries, the rate at which new technologies for exploration, extraction, processing, etc., will be developed, the future actions of foreign suppliers, and so on. Decisionmaking in the materials and energy fields is fraught with particularly high levels of uncertainty.

3. In some cases, the uncertainties relate to possible outcomes that have low probabilities but very high potential costs associated with them. As an illustration, the probability might be considered very slight that our supplies of some critical metal (for which we are almost wholly dependent on imports) will be cut off simultaneously and at short notice by all of our foreign suppliers, but such an event could have devastating effects if it were to happen. Many people, it seems, find it difficult to cope with this kind of uncertainty, and survey responses may be especially hard to interpret.

4. The consequences of many decisions may profoundly affect not only the policymakers' present constituents but also people living elsewhere in the world today and others who are not yet born. In some cases the consequences may be irreversible. For example, the rate at which we consume materials in the United States today potentially has implications both for the present inhabitants of other countries (most notably the poorer countries) and for future generations. Implicitly or explicitly, policymakers must face up to issues of intra- and inter-generational equity, but these are issues that may not be readily dealt with in surveys; furthermore, they raise difficult questions about *who* should be surveyed, given the impossibility of including all those with a stake in the outcome.

Overview of Volume

Beyond the present introduction, this volume consists of three sections: the first discusses basic concepts and issues; the second presents examples of empirical studies; and the third considers the use of research results by policymakers.

Basic Concepts and Issues

The chapter by Farhar-Pilgrim, written primarily for the non-specialist, examines some of the basics of survey research, with a special emphasis on its use for measuring attitudes toward energy. After an introduction to the nature of survey data, the author presents her own discussion of the concept of attitude, and explores the relationships between attitudes and behavior. It is often suggested that attitudes are major determinants of behavior and that by changing attitudes, one might be successful in changing behavior. However, as Farhar-Pilgrim points out (and as discussed again later in the volume), the relationship in reality is rather complex; a correlation certainly seems to exist, but it is not 1.0. Furthermore, it appears that a reverse relationship may also exist; that is, behavior may to some extent be a determinant of attitude.

Farhar-Pilgrim goes on to examine the strengths and limitations of survey data for policymaking; she lists what properly conducted and analyzed surveys can tell us, and what they cannot tell us. If used with caution and to address appropriate questions, she argues, surveys can be very useful; one can have particular confidence if the findings from several different surveys are in agreement.

Finally, she addresses the relevance of survey data to energy policymaking. She makes a distinction between decisions relating to public policy in general and to research policy in particular, and argues that survey findings may be more relevant in connection with policies affecting individual decisions than with those affecting collective decisions.

The authors of Chapter 3 examine a critical assumption underlying the use of surveys to elicit people's values or preferences, namely "the assumption that people know what they want" and that "careful questioning can elicit a faithful representation of them" (i.e., these values). They explore the possibility that a particular topic may have been given little or no attention before the survey takes place, and that the survey itself (and the questions contained therein) may play a major role in attitude formation. The authors go on to suggest that rather than trying - perhaps in vain - to circumvent this problem, it should be openly acknowledged and indeed exploited to obtain a greater insight into the nature of values; they recommend devising "ways to live with uncertainty about what we want."

If people have not thought through what they want in connection with a particular issue, is it appropriate that they should influence policymaking? In the fourth chapter, Miller addresses the question of whose values and attitudes are actually likely to be of interest to policymakers, and introduces a conceptual model for approaching the study of attitudes relating to materials and energy. Basing his discussion on Almond's "pyramid of public opinions", Miller argues that in practice only a small minority of the public are "attentive" on any one particular issue, the rest possessing a poor level of knowledge and holding few structured attitudes. It is the attentive public, he claims, that actually influences policymaking, and he presents evidence suggesting that those who are attentive may hold different views from those who are not. Among his conclusions, Miller suggests that those who wish to influence public policy should attempt to sway the attentive public rather than the mass public.

While the model presented by Miller may be helpful in understanding what frequently happens in practice, his chapter does not address the *desirability* of this process. If the implication is that policymakers *should* consider the views of only the attentive public (i.e., that less emphasis should be placed on surveys of the mass public), I suspect that many would disagree. However, this issue (which raises some basic questions about democracy) is left for the reader to think about.

Empirical Studies

The second section of the book provides some illustrations of the kinds of empirical studies on attitudes toward material and energy resources that are available to policymakers. Much more empirical work has been conducted on energy than on materials, and this is reflected in the offerings presented here.

In the fifth chapter, Melber provides a review of trends in public attitudes toward energy production and conservation alternatives and their relationships to environmental, social, and economic growth issues, as recorded by a series of nationally representative surveys (i.e., public opinion polls) conducted between 1972 and 1979. Among the findings discussed are a reversal of the pre-1973 assumption that growth in energy consumption is a good in itself, the emergence of a dominant view that Americans are wasteful in their consumption patterns, and the existence of considerable disenchantment with many of the currently available energy production options. Although support for environmental protection remains strong, Melber points out, there is some evidence of increasing public willingness to relax a little in this area in return for greater energy availability.

In his chapter on risk assessment, Otway examines direct, explicit attempts to take risks into account in decision-making. He distinguishes between the definition/quantification of risks and public attitudes toward them, and points out that decision makers have traditionally relied on the assumption that quantitatively similar risks (objectively determined) will command a similar level of public acceptance (or non-acceptance). Empirical evidence suggests otherwise, however, for it appears that people's behavior is more likely to be a function of *perceived* risk than of actual risk.

Otway contends that perceived risk can be expressed as an attitude, and suggests that owing to the complexity of relationships between attitudes, beliefs, and behavior, the determinants of risk perception may be many and varied - including non-technical as well as technical factors. He demonstrates the possible importance of non-technical factors by summarizing the results of two empirical studies in which attitudes were measured as functions of underlying beliefs and values. In one study, the respondents were members of the general public (in Austria); in the other study, a group of policymakers were asked to provide both their personal responses and also their perceptions of the responses given by a typical member of the public. The results indicated that non-technical "psychological" aspects did indeed have a greater influence on the public's attitudes than on those of the policymakers; furthermore, the policymakers significantly underestimated the importance of these aspects when role-playing as the public.

Otway concludes his chapter by discussing the uses that regulators, technology-sponsors, and the public might have for risk analyses, given their differing values and beliefs. He warns of the danger of treating the results of risk analysis as scientifically "correct" knowledge on which to base policy decisions, rather than as useful background information or supporting evidence.

In Chapter 6, Warkov addresses the question of whether people's behavior with respect to energy conservation is affected by their time orientation, that is, the way they view the past, present, and future. Warkov's opening review of the literature on this subject suggests the existence of a "complex pattern of relationships that defies simple causal modeling." Warkov himself has examined the behavior of homeowners in deciding to acquire solar hot-water heaters, and his findings reveal that acquisition was most likely to occur if people feared fossil fuel shortages in the future; they were not influenced, it appears, by "implicit appeals to meet one's obligations to society and to future generations" or even by expectations of possible future benefits (such as "insurance against rising fuel prices"). Warkov's personal conclusion is that a combination of the promise of immediate personal benefits, and an appeal based on *fear*, might be the way to persuade people to conserve.

The following two chapters deal with relationships between beliefs, attitudes, and behavior, on the one hand, and underlying human values (as defined by Rokeach) on the other. Having examined the values of a group of people engaged in recycling (assumed to be a form of pro-environmental behavior), Dunlap et al. report that members of this group tend to emphasize such "higher-order" values as aesthetics and self-actualization, while de-emphasizing "lower-order" values such as safety, security, etc. The authors observe that if a person's behavior is indeed linked to his/her value system, it may prove difficult to develop policies to change that behavior since value systems typically seem to depend more on socialization experiences, economic conditions, etc., than on policies. They also suggest that in less affluent times, people are not as likely to engage in pro-environmental behavior unless they see that the issues relate to lower-order needs - as, for example, problems associated with hazardous materials might be related to well-being and security. Consequently, given present difficult economic conditions, they suggest that "policymakers would be wise to emphasize that pollution, resource shortages, and other environmental problems pose direct and serious threats to the health and well-being of the public."

In chapter 9, Rankin reports on a study examining the beliefs, attitudes, and values of three groups of respondents - representing the general public, the neighbors of a nuclear facility, and the members of an environmental group, respectively. On the whole, his findings are not inconsistent with those of Dunlap et al.; he observed that the general public and the nuclear neighbors shared largely similar value systems, while the environmentalists differed significantly in attaching greater importance to certain higher-order values. Rankin's study also revealed that beliefs about energy shortages were little influenced by people's values, while beliefs and attitudes about how to deal with the energy situation were much more value-related.

In considering implications for policymakers, Rankin points out that the ability to quantify environmental values (as now demonstrated) could be helpful in the decision-making process; furthermore, he concludes that by measuring public beliefs early in an energy technology research program, policymakers potentially have the means of predicting how much of an issue they will have to face as the program develops.

Policymakers' Use of Results

The third and final section of the book considers how research results are actually used by policymakers concerned with material and energy resources.

Allen reports on the experience of the federal interagency Resource Conservation Committee, a Cabinet-level panel charged with examining present and proposed federal policies affecting the use/conservation of materials. He mentions various problems that made it difficult for the committee to obtain good data on public attitudes; for example, in the absence of widespread agreement on what is meant by the term "conservation," there was the problem of ensuring that everyone was talking about the same thing; and in general the committee encountered a lack of considered responses regarding extremely complex issues (as might have been expected, based on some of the discussions earlier in this volume).

However, Allen then points out that public officials (both appointed and elected) must take into account a variety of influences in addition to public attitudes, and he concludes by noting that it is not clear how the availability of better attitudinal data in this instance would have affected the committee's deliberations.

Carlson ends the volume by describing the collection and use of energy consumption survey data by the U.S. Department of Energy. She mentions the commissioning of a National Academy of Sciences study in 1976 to assist in determining the major data needs and how they could be collected and utilized by policymakers. Although the importance of attitudinal data was recognized, it was felt that the highest priority should be the establishment of an organized and coherent set of basic statistics on consumption patterns, a task that the Energy Information Administration then proceeded to carry out. With the basic information in hand, program offices and individual utilities have developed specialized surveys relating to particular programs;

these have sometimes included attitudinal questions, such as questions to households about factors affecting their decision making processes and about prefered sources of information (asked in connection with implementation of the Residential Conservation Service mandated by Congress). However, Carlson does not indicate whether or how these attitudinal data have actually been used.

Indeed, firm evidence of the actual use of attitudinal data in policymaking related to energy and materials seems difficult to come by. Perhaps such data are being used, directly or indirectly, but it is simply too difficult to separate out the many different factors which influence how policymakers act; or perhaps, in reality, the data count for little when decisions are being made. As suggested earlier, one can think of many *potential* ways in which the findings of attitudinal research *might* be used. While policymakers cannot be forced to take notice, it seems reasonable to suppose that the researchers might increase their chances of success both by ensuring the right questions are being asked and by assisting in the proper interpretation of the results.

References

Dillman, D.A. (1978), *Mail and Telephone Surveys*, New York: John Wiley and Sons.

McAllister, D. M. (1980), *Evaluation in Environmental Planning*, Cambridge: MIT Press.

Rokeach, M. (1968), *Beliefs, Attitudes and Values*, San Francisco: Jossey-Bass.

Rokeach, M. (1973), *The Nature of Human Values*, New York: Free Press.

Part 1

Concepts, Issues, and Methodological Problems

Barbara Farhar-Pilgrim

2. Surveys: What They Can and Cannot Tell Energy Policymakers

Abstract[1]

This chapter provides the non-behavioral scientist with an introduction to the strengths and limitations of attitudinal research, including a discussion of what is known about the interrelationships between attitudes and behavior, and a discussion of what surveys can and cannot tell us. The relevance of survey results to policy making, especially in the field of energy, is discussed.

Introduction

For eight years, the American people have been confronted by "the energy crisis." Plentiful energy had shaped the society they lived in, from suburbia, highways, and automation to consumer goods. After experiencing unconstrained growth in the 1960s, the United States in 1973 suddenly faced increased gasoline and oil prices, long lines at gas stations, decreased speed limits, and calls for energy conservation. These sudden events (compounded by severe winters causing job losses and other social disruptions, and by droughts decreasing the supply of hydropower) made the nation more aware of its dependence on energy, and energy policy an increasingly important government activity.

Carefully collected public opinion data can be relevant for government policymaking in energy. Although private industry has long recognized the importance of corporate and product "image" in the public mind, government at all levels seems peculiarly resistant to the use of attitudinal data. Policy is a stimulus to evoke a behavioral response. For purposes of any given policy decision, public opinion can be viewed more as a parameter for than as a target of policy. Since behavior is correlated to attitudes, policies that ignore or are in conflict with public attitudes are unlikely to evoke the desired response unless coercion mandates compliance.[2]

The nation's energy dilemma is interwoven into the fabric of its economic and social life. Virtually no one contests the fact that Americans are wasteful of energy and that the importation of oil is developing into a serious national problem through its impact on the balance of trade, the strength of the dollar, and its implications for international relations. Energy conservation through a variety of means has been heralded by the federal government and adopted by corporations and individuals with measurable effects, but only a small fraction of the conservation potential has yet been realized. The conservation of energy is national policy. The effectiveness of energy conservation and renewable resource measures in partially supplying the nation's energy depends largely on what people know, feel, and do about it.

This chapter is organized into two parts: a discussion for the non-behavioral scientist of the strengths and limitations of attitudinal research, and consideration of the policy relevance of survey research, especially for energy policy.

Understanding Surveys

In understanding data on public opinion about energy in the United States, several points should be kept in mind. A survey is an attempt to measure and aggregate the variegated and segmented opinions of the polity. Opinion is segmented by a variety of factors: group affiliations, geographical region, social class, occupation, and so on. Each individual is situated in a particular social milieu and thus experiences the environment differently. Experiences affecting an individual's opinion of whether an energy crisis actually exists can include, for example, whether one's own schools and factories are closed due to fuel shortages, whether gasoline is readily available, whether and to what extent utility bills increase, and what information is available to the individual.

Further, individuals vary in their personal responses to these experiences. Two individuals living in approximately the same life circumstances can respond in completely different ways -- one might view an energy crisis as an exciting challenge to creative ability and altruistic motives; another might perceive it to be a serious threat and seek to deny its existence. Survey findings can be used more effectively when one is aware of these complexities. Maintaining common sense and avoiding truisms about "the public" also enhance an accurate perception of public sentiment about the nation's energy situation.

In the remainder of this section, the nature of survey data is discussed. The concept "attitude" is defined and its relationship to action or behavior[3] described. Public opinion is distinguished from private opinion, and the importance of this distinction is discussed.

Surveys of public opinion tell us only part of what we need to know about people and energy. That part is significant when it is the product of sound methods, but it does not yield the complete story about the human dimensions of energy. Survey research has shortcomings and limitations, but it also has strengths. As Deutscher (1973:5) has observed, "We do not discard reports because of biases or flaws of one sort or another. If we did, there would be no history."

Surveys

A survey is a snapshot. It momentarily "stops the action" of the ongoing life of thought and sentiment. The quality of the information contained in a survey, as in a photograph -- its focus, accuracy, clarity, and lucidity -- depends in part on the skill of the survey researcher (or photographer) and in part on his methods and tools (cameras, film, instruments). The survey snapshot gives us a description of public opinion at one point in time. Even longitudinal data (collected at specific time intervals) provide only a succession of shapshots, not enough to make a moving picture.

When carefully collected, survey data can be descriptive of an entire population, providing systematic and comparable empirical data that can be quantified and analyzed. But what is the nature of the empirical data that can be collected through a survey? Generally, surveys of public opinion purport to measure attitudes, beliefs, definitions of the situation, knowledge and information sources, behavioral intention, and, sometimes, behavior. They also gather information on sociodemographic variables, such as age, gender, and level of education.

Attitudes and Their Relationship to Action

An attitude is a predisposition to action. If a person feels positively toward an object (person, place, thing) then s/he is likely to behave positively toward it. The converse also holds.

Attitude has cognitive, affective, and behavioral elements. Cognitive implies some descriptive and analytical knowledge about the object (person, place, thing, behavior, idea, process) with respect to which the attitude is held. Affective refers to the feeling content of the attitude, how intense (or salient) the attitude is, and whether the emotion is positive or antipathetic. Behavioral elements are the verbal expressions of the attitude, and, sometimes, the motive link between attitude and action.

As Linn (1965:353) has pointed out, scientific debate continues over the definition of attitude and related concepts, such as opinion, beliefs, sentiments, sets, evaluations and intentions.

> One of the most diversely defined concepts in social psychology is attitude. Not only are there vast differences concerning what properly constitutes an attitude, but there has been developing a large literature debating how attitudes should be measured.

Some researchers have distinguished attitude and belief (Dillman, 1978; Fishbein, 1967). In this distinction, attitudes are defined as evaluative, describing how people feel about something. Beliefs are defined as what people think is true or false. For purposes of this discussion, attitude is used more broadly to subsume these various definitions. A more detailed list of what surveys can and cannot be used to measure is provided later in the chapter. A verbal response to a questionnaire or interview item is behavior (verbal behavior) which is thought to be an observable index of attitude.

A controversy has been raging in sociology, psychology, and political science for at least 40 years about the relationship between what people say and what they do. Public opinion surveys and techniques of attitude scaling which use statistics and computing capabilities were developed, and this in turn permitted speedy processing of vastly greater amounts of data than previously possible (Babbie, 1973; Guttman, 1944; Lazarsfeld, 1948; Likert, 1932; Osgood, 1969; Thurstone and Chave, 1929). An extensive literature emerged on known problems in attitude measurement and scaling[4] particularly related to the issue of predicting behavior from these measurements. In fact, Deutscher (1973:149) stated flatly, "Responses to formal interviews inform us about behavior in a formal interviewing situation and little else."

The second source of concern was that much of the literature attempting to relate attitudes to behavior dealt with the relationship between racial prejudice and overt discrimination (e.g., LaPiere, 1935; DeFleur and Westie, 1958; Linn, 1965; Merton, 1940). Clearly, the problem of racial discrimination was perceived as a problem of the attitudes and behavior of individuals rather than as a social problem. The discrepancy observed between attitude and behavior in race relations was termed "hypocrisy." However, to describe the social world accurately (as a physical scientist seeks to describe the physical world and a biologist the biological world), a social researcher is well advised to minimize personal impact on the natural processes being observed. The relationship between attitude and action is an empirically observable phenomenon. Society needs to know more about what is before it can intelligently assess how to go about changing itself.

The evidence suggests that a correlation between attitude and action is defensible on the basis of social science findings, but that correlation most definitely is not 1.0; many factors other than attitudes influence what people ultimately do. Some of the reasons for differences between attitudes and action are described below. These explanations of the observed discrepancy fall into two related categories: (1) problems in theoretical constructs and (2) problems in the measurement of attitudes and behavior.

Problems in Theoretical Constructs

Attitude and action have different characteristics, such that measuring and comparing them contain elements of the classic apples/oranges problem. Action has been differentiated into verbal responses and overt actions. Deutscher (1966) stressed the nonverbal aspects of behavior when attempting to compare words with deeds. However, a very large proportion of significant social behavior is symbolic, and this verbal behavior represents a gray area in the attitude-behavior dichotomy. As Jones and Harris (1967:1) have noted, "When a person verbalizes an opinion he may or may not hold an underlying attitude that 'corresponds' to that opinion." Jones and Harris demonstrated in a laboratory experiment that people perceived someone as expressing a "true" underlying attitude when they saw the social situation was not coercing any particular point of view.[5] Schuman and Johnson (1976) distinguished "elicited verbal attitudes" from "spontaneous verbal attitudes." Elicited attitudes are responses to questionnaires, interviews, or other direct measurement methods. Spontaneous attitudes are expressions of opinion that emerge in everyday conversations with friends and others. Schuman and Johnson considered spontaneous attitudes a form of behavior. "Attitude" as discussed in the literature and as used in this chapter refers to elicited attitudes.

Public and private opinions. One of the more important distinctions in helping to understand the mixed empirical evidence was that drawn by Deutscher (1973) between public and private opinions. This distinction can readily be observed in everyday life in the difference between private opinions shared among intimates and opinions stated openly and publicly. The survey interview or questionnaire situation was succinctly summarized in the following passage:

> The respondent is urged to reveal his most private opinions on an object without relating it to any other objects, or placing it in any context, with the assurance that the interviewer doesn't care what he says and no one else will ever know he said it (Deutscher, 1973:149).

Private opinions become public when people can express themselves collectively with anonymity, as in purchasing decisions and voting. In most of social life, utterances are treated as public and consequences follow from them. Feelings are frequently masked for purposes of reputation, politics, economic gain, prestige, and maintenance of norms. All manner of common impulses to action are suppressed and even repressed.[6] Clearly, the survey with its promises of confidentiality and anonymity is designed to elicit private opinion.[7] The question is, what relationship do these private opinions have to public opinion and to action?

A marked congruence has been noted in the social science literature between attitude (as measured in surveys) and specific behaviors such as voting, buying habits, and leisure time activities, which are the collective actions of individuals, not the organized action of groups or committees. To quote Deutscher (1966:247):

> It would be a serious selective distortion of the existing evidence to suggest that all of it indicates an incongruence between what people say and what they do. Consumers sometimes do change their buying habits in ways they say they will, people frequently vote as they tell pollsters they will, urban relocation populations

> may accurately predict to interviewers the type of housing they will obtain, local party politicians do in fact employ the campaign tactics which they believe to be most effective, and youngsters will provide survey researchers with reports of their own contact or lack of contact with the police which are borne out by police records.

Even so, there still exists much of the significance in social life that is constrained by factors other than attitudinal, and it is to be expected that public opinion survey data would be less useful in increasing understanding in those areas. One critical variable is social support, described below.

Social support. Social support variables affecting behavior which have been established in the literature are as follows: group size, cohesiveness, status, frequency of interaction, group power membership, group identification, visibility of behavior, and legitimacy of group norms (Liska, 1974). These variables are frequently measured by asking how the respondent's coworkers or spouse feels about the attitude object. The opinions of groups with which the respondent identifies (such as family, work groups, and reference groups), especially of the "opinion leaders" of those groups, and of significant others can affect individual attitudes. In short, individuals are likely to have the same attitudes as those of other members of groups with which they identify.

As sophistication in analysis has increased, multivariate techniques have permitted the statistical manipulation of more than one attitudinal variable, with weighting techniques employed. When multivariate analyses are used, the question arises as to whether attitudes and other effects on behavior, such as social support, are merely additive or interactive.

One approach to the social support variable is to treat it as an intervening variable in a consistency model. If social support is congruent with attitudes, it should reinforce the effects of attitudes on behavior in a given situation. If it is not congruent, it will counterbalance attitudes and decrease attitude-behavior consistency (Liska, 1974).

A second approach is to treat attitudes and social support as equivalent variables in accounting for the behavioral outcome. Empirical evidence has suggested that attitudes are more important than social support in accounting for behavior in competitive situations, and social support is the more important variable in cooperative situations (Liska, 1974).

A third approach, the interaction model, has received less empirical support than the additive model. This model assumes that neither attitude nor social support has an independent effect on behavior, but that the effect of one depends on the level of the other. While the attitude-behavior controversy is far from settled, an interaction model used with multiple attitude measures points to a direction for future investigation that takes full advantage of conceptual advances and multivariate techniques to increase the power of analyses.

Problems in Measurement

Deutscher (1973) reviewed three studies on the attitude-behavior relationship conducted at three points in time over a 30-year period.[8] He argued that the three studies, all of which had been methodologically criticized, demonstrated the lack of correlation between attitude and action. Rebutting this position, Ajzen et al. (1970) argued that none of the three studies actually measured the attitude-behavior relationship. Ajzen et al. showed that the three studies compared attitude toward an object with behavioral intention and behavioral intention with behavior, but none compared attitude toward an object with behavior toward that object.

Several other methodological problems offering explanations for the apparent discrepancy between attitude and action in the empirical literature have been suggested. These include: (1) "cutting corners" by interviewers and coders (Roth, 1965); (2) "social desirability," which is the observed inclination of respondents to strive for the "right answer" (Taylor, 1961); (3) "acquiescence response sets," which is the tendency exhibited by some respondents to go along with anything presented (Taylor, 1961); and (4) the existence of different kinds of attitudes and acts. Further, Deutscher (1973:91) argued that the very notion of simple linear cause-and-effect relationships has "by and large been discarded in the philosophy of science."

Liska (1974) also pointed out several reasons for the discrepant findings. When the social object of the attitude is unfamiliar, attitudes may be poorly formed, thus reducing their impact on behavior. Another problem is that, when attitudes are measured at the same level of generality as behavior, they are more predictive of behavior but this "generality equivalence" is difficult to achieve. Generality equivalence refers to the framing of items on attitude and behavior so that they are at the same level of specificity or generality. For example, instead of asking, "How do you feel about solar energy -- do you favor or oppose it?", one would ask, "How do you feel about using solar energy on your home?" when comparing attitude to behavioral intention ("Do you have any plans to install solar energy on your home in the next 2-3 years? Have you taken any actions, such as getting cost estimates?") or behavior ("Do you presently have a solar energy system in your home?"). Liska also cited as a methodological difficulty the "play-like atmosphere" of attitude measurement situations. He concluded that the issue of the attitude-behavior relationship remained unsolved.

Attitude Change

We have been discussing how attitudes affect behavior, but a major theoretical school of thought in social psychology has centered on the reverse relationship, how behavior affects attitudes. Three explanatory schemes, though not identical, have the same fundamental notion in common -- that of the impetus for consistency between attitudes and action. These are the theory of cognitive dissonance (Festinger, 1957), balance theory (Rosenberg, et. al., 1960), and the congruity model (Osgood, Suci, and Tannenbaum, 1957). The fundamental notion is that action inconsistent with attitudes is a force for attitude change. Action that is consistent with attitudes is held to produce a state of psychic equilibrium. Action that is inconsistent with attitudes is held to produce a state of disequilibrium, imbalance, or cognitive dissonance. Dissonance is "a state of psychological discomfort or tension which motivates efforts to achieve consonance" (Brown, 1965:584). For example, a person may be in the position of realizing, "I smoke cigarettes" and "smoking cigarettes is dangerous to life." Or, "I support Edward Kennedy" and "I am opposed to national health insurance."

The state of tension or strain resulting from cognitive dissonance is thought to result in cognitive shifts to bring attitudes into consonance with behavior. A relatively low tolerance for ambiguity is implied. It follows that if people change their behavior, their attitudes will eventually "fall into line." This notion has been empirically supported (see, for example, King and Janis, 1956).

In the case of the examples above, a smoker might change his attitudes toward smoking and eventually stop smoking, or the person might search for evidence that smoking is not dangerous to health. The Kennedy supporter might alter his views on national health insurance or withdraw support for the Kennedy candidacy.

The implication of consistency theory is that if behavior is changed, attitudes will afterward become more consistent with the action taken. Behavior itself may be more amenable to change through government appeals in certain situations. A person might reduce the thermostat setting to 65° because the President appealed to all citizens do this, and energy conserving attitudes with further related behavior might follow later on. Consistency theory implies that while attitudes may be causally related to behavior, behavior may also be causally related to attitudes. A feedback loop between attitudes and action may be the most accurate way to describe their relationship.

Summary

Schuman and Johnson (1976:199) concluded from a recent extensive review of the attitude-behavior controversy literature and empirical studies:

> Our review has shown that most attitude-behavior studies yield positive results. The correlations that do occur are large enough to indicate that important causal forces are involved . . . . They are rarely large enough to suggest that attitudinal responses can serve as mechanical substitutes for behavioral measures . . . . This is not to deny that there are important areas where attitudinal measures are largely unrelated to behavior, but these should be seen as interesting cases that reveal something special about social life -- e.g., that the behavior in question is performed with little awareness or informed anticipation or that social constraints on behavior are of exceptional power. Such findings do not mean that attitude and behavior are unrelated.

The authors felt that, while social support can help clarify the attitude-behavior relationship, perhaps greater insight would result from "constructing variations in the situation of action" and asking for "personal definitions of the situation." They noted that the "current emphasis on attribution theory in social psychology (Jones et al., 1972) can be seen as an experimental reorientation in the direction of studying personal perspectives" (p. 202).

In summary, survey data have certain limitations, such as problems of theory and measurement. Nevertheless, attitudes are held to be causally related to action, although they do not fully explain behavior. It is therefore of significance to understand attitudes when attempting to understand behavior.

Strengths and Limitations of Survey Data for Policymaking

Because a policymaker is not a behavioral scientist, s/he needs to be made aware of what survey data can and cannot be expected to describe. An important dichotomy relevant to what survey data can and cannot tell us relates to different levels of action in society. Although each person's opinion may carry equal weight in a public opinion poll, that person assuredly does not carry such weight in influencing policy, implementing decisions or other ways. For decisions and actions within the purview of the individual actor, such as what home to buy, what college to attend, or what candidate to support, the results of opinion surveys are directly relevant to the action in question. However, for decisions of national policy, allocation of tax monies, location of major projects, and the like, survey data are only partially relevant because these decisions are made at the systemic rather than at the individual level.

Data other than public opinion polls must be collected to gain a more comprehensive understanding of social processes relevant to energy issues. Employing different measurements and independent sources of information on the same phenomenon improves the accuracy of knowledge and the degree of confidence in it (Webb et al., 1977).

What Surveys Can Tell Us

Properly analyzed, survey data can be used to describe relationships among variables and the strength of these relationships, to test hypothesized relationships, and to generate multivariate analyses with which to draw causal inferences concerning predictor and dependent variables. They can describe populations. They permit limited prediction of certain classes of behavior (buying decisions, voting, religious observation, leisure time activity) for the population as a whole or for any particular individual within it. Certain classes of individuals may be predicted to be more likely to behave in specified ways than other classes of individuals. The survey provides sound empirical data descriptive of population segments. On the basis of survey data, it is possible to say that people are more likely to do

X than Y if we know their attitudes with respect to X and Y, but we cannot say this with a probability value.

Assuming sound methodology, survey data can provide accurate descriptions for the sampled population within the sociopolitical context at a given time on the following kinds of variables:

- attitude toward the idea of an object in the abstract or in *general* (person, place, thing, idea, practice, and the like), favorable or unfavorable;
- attitude toward or evaluation of a *specific* object (favorability or opposition, yes or no, for or against);
- perceptions of reality; beliefs about what is real, true, moral, factual;
- levels of knowledge, both subjectively assessed and objectively tested;
- sources of information used, frequency of contact, and credibility of information sources;
- preferences and wishes;
- fears and concerns; and
- certain sociodemographic information (e.g., gender and level of education).

With somewhat less accuracy, survey data can also tell us:

- salience of an object; importance, priorities;
- other (more sensitive) sociodemographic information (e.g., income);
- actual behavior (action already taken);
- needs; and
- reasons for opinions; rationales.

These latter variables are more subject to measurement problems and respondent/interviewer difficulties such as forgetting, lying, selective inattention, desire to please, desire to impress, inability to distinguish needs from desires or to articulate needs clearly, difficulty in knowing why one feels as one does, and difficulty in item validity.

Survey data are accurate and valid to a greater or lesser degree according to the sensitivity of the topic of the survey. Surveys have been conducted on a vast array of topics, but it is to be expected that findings from surveys on political attitudes and behavior more accurately describe the population than surveys on, for example, sexual attitudes and behavior. Attitudes on sensitive topics, being emotionally laden, are much more difficult for the respondent to articulate.

What Surveys Cannot Tell Us

- Survey data cannot be used to tell us what the important questions are.
- They cannot tell us what a given individual will do in many situations.
- They do not permit us to predict with any degree of confidence how attitudes will change at some future time.
- They cannot inform us as to the effectiveness of or public response to any particular project or policy decision, since these are subject to political forces beyond public opinion.
- They cannot be used to describe or reveal processes at the social system level.
- They cannot project future policy issues or decisions.
- They cannot predict what the totality of individual actions will be in certain classes of behavior, especially in fad or fashion and in nonroutine situations.

Further cautions are required in understanding the value of surveys for policy. Item results can be affected by whether items are open-ended or forced choice, by item wording, and by the placement of the item in the context of other items in the instrument. Findings can also be affected by sampling problems and interviewers. The results from any one item in any given survey should be viewed only tentatively. Enough technical problems of measurement exist that only when items have been replicated can a pattern of response be said to exist. Further, use of several items in a survey to measure the same attitude or opinion with comparable results is a much stronger treatment than the use of a single item (Scott, 1968).

Caution is necessary in settling on a finding when only one item or survey produces a given result. Just because no findings contradictory to that item exist, it is still tentative. When contradictory findings do exist, unless interpretation is possible to account for the contradiction, no conclusion is possible. When findings from several surveys are not contradictory but instead reveal a pattern, it can be concluded that the empirical evidence has revealed a social fact.

In the strictest sense, the aggregation of survey items that do not replicate each other is not considered scientifically valid. Hypotheses cannot legitimately be tested in this way. Nevertheless, in organizing a body of empirical knowledge, it is extremely useful to search out patterns of findings, which produce a partial test of convergent validity. When a major purpose of the exercise is to produce social science information of interest to the policymaker, such aggregation is essential and necessary. This approach also provides information relevant to the social researcher by aiding the formulation of hypotheses and the replication of previous work and, thus, the cumulation of knowledge.

Research and polling customs have developed in such a way that anyone embarking on a study of any topic is free to devise his or her own items (within the bounds of sound technique). While this approach results in findings not strictly comparable and thus not directly assisting systematic accumulation of empirical evidence, it does offer certain advantages. Given the expense of survey data collection and analysis, a policy of total replication would obliterate much of the freshness and variety provided by numerous researchers exploring problems. The existing diversity in studies is a strength on the national scale.

Relevance to Energy Policy

In their review of the literature on attitudes toward nuclear energy, Melber et al., (1977:305) stated that ". . . public poll data carefully gathered, compared, and evaluated, can perform an important function in providing public input to the (energy policy) decision process." However, they warn:

> As far as we know, no one has yet argued that public policy decisions are primarily determined by public opinions. In fact, this seems particularly unlikely in the case of energy policy decisions because there appear to be so many real constraints on the course that energy decisions *can* take (p. 303).

The salience of public opinion, and thus of survey findings, for policy varies by the kind and level of policy decision making. The development and adoption of nuclear energy is a collective adoption decision. Such decisions are very different in character from an individual decision to purchase solar heating or engage in energy conservation activities. As a result, data on public opinion are more directly relevant to policies pertaining to individual decisions such as energy conservation and residential use of solar energy. Organizations such as utilities and industries decide about the use of nuclear energy or industrial process heat. Table 1 summarizes the structural location of adoption decision making for each energy source. It should be kept in mind, however, that national policy (e.g., tax incentives) can affect individual adoption decision making.

Because public opinion is more directly relevant to some policy decisions than others, it is useful to distinguish two types of policy decision making: those decisions involving (1) public policy and (2) research policy. Public policy decisions pertain to the creation and allocation of public monies for the administration of the government, social control and sanctions, defense, and public welfare. Research policy decisions, which are usually thought to be a subset of public policy, entail the allocation and expenditure of public funds to support basic and applied scientific investigations into general and specific topics of concern. The choice of research topics and the emphasis given to each in the distribution of resources constitute a major policy decision process occurring at the national level. For example, the federal investment in research on nuclear energy constituted a series of major national policy decisions.

The allocation of government support to research in solar energy is a research policy decision; the creation of tax incentives and information programs is a public policy decision. Survey research is ordinarily more oriented to questions of public policy than research policy. Survey findings reveal public preferences on policy alternatives such as price increases, rationing of energy supplies, and tax incentives. Public opinion polls on nuclear plants tend to be addressed to the general problem of whether the public will tolerate nuclear plants and how the public feels about the idea of nuclear energy in general, but not to specific plans or behavioral options. Studies on energy conservation and solar energy would include individual plans and behavioral choices.

This is not to say that survey research is irrelevant to policymakers concerned about research policy and collec-

Table 1. Level of Adoption Decision Making by Type of Energy Source

Type of Energy Source	Individual	Organizational	Collective*
Nuclear		X	X
Fusion		X	X
Natural Gas	**	X	X
Coal		X	X
Oil	**	X	X
Solar energy, decentralized	X	X***	
Solar energy, centralized		X	
Energy conservation	X	X	

*Includes community, nation. Adoption decisions are affected by regulatory procedures.

**Natural gas and oil may be viewed as within the purview of individual homeowner decisionmaking. Pragmatically, however, in both new and used housing stock, decisions about heating systems are ordinarily made by the companies originally producing homes. Exceptions to this would be the custom housing and new furnace markets.

***Adoption of decentralized solar technologies can also occur by builders/developers, architectural firms, etc.

tive alternatives. Melber et al. (1977) listed the following benefits to policymakers from survey findings on nuclear energy: (1) a broader perspective than that put forward by special interest groups; (2) forewarning of implementation problems; (3) need for improved information distribution; (4) need for more productive mechanisms for resolving disputes; and (5) stimulus for new and more socially acceptable solutions to problems that have risen. The authors indicated that "good" energy decisions are guided by social values. The utility of survey data for policy decisions on collective alternatives, such as nuclear energy, concerns social values more and individual behavior less. The relationship between public opinion and collective adoption (Farhar et. al., 1978) is indirect, finding expression that affects policy outcomes only through actions of citizen activists and other collectivity channels. It is precisely here that "private opinion" becomes relevant, because the anonymous, permissive expression of opinion encouraged by the interview setting, to the degree that it is successful in eliciting an expression of honest attitude without the constraint of social variables prohibiting such expression, permits description of what ultimately will affect outcomes. Constrained emotion does not disappear, but seeks an outlet for its expression. Thus, the information revealed in surveys describes the emotional milieu in which a given policy thrives or withers.

Survey data on the use of solar energy and energy conservation are more closely linked to behavior than for other energy sources, since the kinds of behaviors involved in adopting each involve individual action. Survey data are less directly linked to organizational adoption decisions, such as utility adoption of solar energy as a centralized energy source, although they can indicate the popularity of an organizational action. They are useful in describing the social acceptability of policies to encourage or discourage solar energy and energy conservation. With any innovative topic such as solar energy, however, the usefulness of survey data on policy preferences may be limited by low levels of knowledge on the part of the population at large, many of whom are unaware of the implications of various policy alternatives and unfamiliar with the social and economic implications of new technologies. They can say whether it "sounds like a good idea," but they cannot say how they will feel about it when they know more or have experienced it.

Another important contribution to policy from survey data is the description of the perceived world as a social fact. In the physical world, oil may be discovered in Texas but not in Minnesota. A policymaker may be pleased that Texas's energy supply problems are solved for the moment, and he is likely to view the Minnesota energy supply situation as a problem to be solved. He accepts the limitations of the *physical* world without question -- it is difficult to argue with Mother Nature. But if he learns that running large power lines diagonally across the state of Minnesota is not socially acceptable, he may become very angry at the existence of a *social* limitation.

Whether the policymaker believes that the public is right or wrong, a fount of wisdom or misguided and shortsighted, ultimately what people want will affect outcomes, and coercive measures go only a certain distance in gaining compliance with or tolerance of undesired policies. A great deal of public money has been spent on what ultimately proved to be socially unacceptable policies. What is widely perceived to be most desirable or least harmful should be of great interest to any policymaker, not only in his or her own self-interest, but also from a professional point of view.

It is important to understand that attitudes about energy and energy policy options can be affected by a variety of related but indirect factors, such as who is promoting the policy. If the President is recommending a certain line of action on energy, and an individual dislikes the President, that person will be disinclined to support the policy. Emanating from some other more acceptable source, the policy might be acceptable. Therefore, public opinion on policy alternatives are inseparable from the organizations and persons who stand for them. Further, as Phillips (1978) pointed out, attitudes toward other topics can affect attitudes toward energy policy. For example, pollsters had been reporting "somewhat improving" public attitudes toward major corporations during 1977 and 1978. This improvement in attitude probably affected how the public viewed major oil and energy companies and their role in the nation's energy problems. Phillips argued that President Carter's rebukes of oil companies did little to enhance the political chances of his own energy package at that time.

A variety of factors beyond public attitudes can affect the social acceptability of a policy or a technology. Scott and Shore (1974) distinguished "tractable" and "intractable" variables.[9] Policy decisions can affect tractable variables; intractable variables are those which cannot be directly affected by policy decisions and their implementation. The distinction is not based on qualities inherent in variables themselves, but in their relationship to the policy. For example, in their research on the negative income tax, "sense of internal fate control" was well established in the literature as relevant to poverty, but Scott and Shore considered it intractable. The relationship of age and poverty, however, presented a variable, age, that could be taken into account in program policy. Similarly, attitudes toward energy issues are intractable variables not directly amenable to change through policy decisions. However, other variables, such as levels of awareness, may be more tractable. Further research is needed to define these.

Lopreato and Meriwether (1976) suggested that knowledge of regional differences in energy matters, given recent pressure for regionalization, would be helpful to policymakers. These differences include energy sources, consumption behavior, prices, and attitudes. Perlman and Warren (1977) conducted a comparative study of families responding to the energy crisis in Oregon, Connecticut, and Alabama. They indicated that policy alternatives are supported or opposed by various groups in American society depending largely on how they perceive their interests to be affected by the interests of the main regions of the nation and by the interests of particular industries, especially the automobile industry. Perlman and Warren found that economic production is of paramount importance to energy decision makers, environmental concerns were of less importance, and equity was an even less powerful constraint on policy. Equity was defined as "the attempt to distribute costs and benefits of public policy in appropriately fair increments across various socioeconomic segments of the population" (p. 172). Survey data permitted the researchers to discover that a disproportionate negative impact of energy shortages had been suffered by those in lowest economic groups, minorities, and the aged. An increase in energy prices particularly disadvantages those with annual incomes below $15,000. If social equity is a national value, then this information should be important to policymakers in choosing among energy policy options.

Phillips (1978) analyzed President Carter's energy program in light of available public opinion data, and concluded:

> The public did not react enthusiastically . . . because major elements of that program were at odds with majority viewpoints on matters so fundamental to American politics as growth *versus* energy conservation, production incentives *versus* income redistribution, and on the relative role of federal regulation (p. 14).

Deutscher (1966) asserted that the policymaker "as a man of

action . . . is interested in overt *behavior*," and especially in behavioral changes.

> We cannot blandly suggest to the policymaker that if he changes behavior, a change in attitude will follow. Nor can we lead him to assume that if he can alter attitudes, he need only wait patiently for the appropriate behavior to develop (p. 252).

Public policy is a stimulus designed to evoke a behavioral response. Since behavior is correlated to attitudes, policies that fly in the face of public attitudes are unlikely to evoke the desired behavioral response unless coercion mandates compliance. Survey data on citizen attitudes, beliefs, definitions of the situation, knowledge, fears and concerns, and preferences provide a fundamental framework against which policy options can and should be assessed.

Policymakers can also discover whether a policy idea is popular. A survey can be used to discern whether policies, such as gasoline rationing or tax incentives, are accepted by the public. Policymakers can discover through surveys whether a policy "worked" through self-reports of behavioral response. They can learn the public's behavioral intentions at a given point in time, their definition of the relative importance of things, and their preferences for various options, all of which are directly relevant to assessing the social desirability of any given policy option.

Concluding Observations

Analysis of survey data has revealed that, overall, most studies on energy opinion are atheoretical (Farhar et al., 1979; Unseld and Crews, 1979). This limits their usefulness for policy purposes and perpetuates research gaps. Theory is supposed to describe and explain the real world, which is information the effective policymaker needs.

From the few theoretical analyses which have been done, the following hypotheses for further research are suggested:

- that willingness to conserve energy, adopt solar energy, and accept other alternatives, such as nuclear power or gasoline rationing, are a function of belief in an energy crisis;

- that belief in an energy crisis is a function of (a) attribution of the energy problem to the declining availability of fossil fuels rather than to sociopolitical and economic causes; (b) negative energy-related impacts experienced or anticipated; (c) awareness of energy facts and issues; (d) environmental concern; and (e) exposure to credible information sources with high levels of factual knowledge;

- that adoption of energy conserving practices and of solar energy is a function of (a) their perceived effectiveness; (b) concern about any risks involved; (c) assessment of the relative advantage of doing so; (d) awareness and knowledge; (e) a favorable position toward it; (f) the availability of the necessary information and equipment; and (g) coming to a decision to act.

Eight years have elapsed since the 1973 oil embargo. It has become increasingly clear since then that energy prices are rising and oil imports continue to be necessary. Energy-related problems have not been solved, nor are they likely to be solved, in such a way that the nation can return to the era of inexpensive and plentiful sources of power. The success of what policymakers and the public do about this situation will depend in part on the congruence of their respective analyses of it and of the desirability of various alternative solutions. Despite the plurality of views, some common ground needs to be found for assessment of the situation and ways to deal with it. Inevitably, trade-offs will be involved; information is needed on the balance to be achieved in the complex question of what is possible, what is acceptable, and what is optimal.

Notes

[1]This work was carried out under the National Study of the Residential Solar Consumer at the Solar Energy Research Institute.

[2]The Susan B. Anthony dollar may be an interesting example of failure to take public attitudes into account. Pretesting the dollar's design in the field would have alerted policymakers to the fact that many businesses find them inconvenient and refuse to use them.

[3]The terms "action" and "behavior" are used interchangeably.

[4]See, for example, Babbie, 1973; Merton, 1940.

[5]This lack of constraint in the social setting in which

an opinion is being expressed is the hallmark of the survey interview.

[6]Much psychotherapy is conducted with the direct purpose of putting people "in touch" with their own feelings.

[7]The problem of purposeful lying does not appear to be widespread, although it is known to occur.

[8]The studies reviewed were LaPiere (1935), DeFleur and Westie (1958), and Linn (1965).

[9]Tractable variables have also been termed "manipulable" through policy action.

References

Ajzen, I., R.K. Darroch, M. Fishbein and J.A. Hornik (1970), "Looking Backward Revisited: A Reply to Deutscher," *Amer. Soc.*, *5*, 267-272.

Babbie, Earl R. (1973), *Survey Research Methods*. Belmont: Wadsworth Publ. Co.

Brown, Roger (1965), *Social Psychology*. New York: The Free Press.

De Fleur, M.L. and F.R. Westie (1958), "Verbal Attitudes and Overt Acts: An Experiment on the Salience of Attitudes," *Am. Soc. Rev.*, 23, 667-673.

Deutscher, Irwin (1973), *What We Say/What We Do*. Glenview: Scott, Foresman and Co.

Deutscher, Irwin (1966), "Words and Deeds: Social Science and Social Policy," *Soc. Probs.*, *13*, 235-265.

Dillman, Don (1978), *Mail and Telephone Surveys*. New York: John Wiley & Sons.

Farhar, B.C., P. Weis, C.T. Unseld, B.A. Burns (1979), *Public Opinion About Energy*: *A Literature Review*. SERI/TR-53-155, Golden: Solar Energy Research Institute, June.

Farhar, B.C., G. Johnson, J.A. Clark, J. Mewes, R. Rinkle and S. Shoulders (1978), *Technology and Society*: *Weather Modification in South Dakota*. Boulder: Institute of Behavioral Science, University of Colorado, December.

Festinger, Leon (1957), *A Theory of Cognitive Dissonance*. New York: Row, Peterson.

Fishbein, Martin (1967), "A Consideration of Beliefs, and Their Role in Attitude Measurement," *Readings in Attitude Theory and Measurement*. Ed., M. Fishbein, New York: John Wiley & Sons, 257-266.

Guttman, L. (1944), "A Basis for Scaling Quantitative Data," *Am. Soc. Rev., 9*, 139-150.

Jones, Edward E. and Victor A. Harris (1967), "The Attribution of Attitudes," *J. Exp. Soc. Psych., 3*, 1-24.

Jones, E.E. et al. (1972), *Attribution: Perceiving the Causes of Behavior*. Morristown, N.J.: General Learning Press.

King, B.T. and I.L. Janis (1956), "Comparison of the Effectiveness of Improvised Versus Nonimprovised Role-Playing in Producing Opinion Changes," *Human Relations, 9*, 177-186.

LaPiere, Richard T. (1935), "Attitudes vs. Actions," *Social Forces, 13*, 230-237.

Lazarsfeld, Paul F. (1948), *The People's Choice*. New York: Columbia Univ. Press.

Likert, R. (1932), "A Technique for the Measurement of Attitudes," *Archives of Psych., 22*, 5-55.

Linn, Lawrence S. (1965), "Verbal Attitudes and Overt Behavior: A Study of Racial Discrimination," *Social Forces, 43*, 353-364.

Liska, Allen E. (1974), "Emergent Issues in the Attitude-Behavior Consistency Controversy," *Am. Soc. Rev., 39*, 261-272.

Lopreato, S.C. and M.W. Meriwether (1976), *Energy Attitudinal Surveys: Summary, Annotations, Research Recommendations*. Austin: Univ. of Texas.

Melber, B., S. Nealey, J. Hammersla and W. Rankin (1977), *Nuclear Power and the Public: Analysis of Collected Survey Research*. Seattle: Battelle Memorial Institute, November.

Merton, R.K. (1940), "Fact and Fictitiousness in Ethnic Opinionnaires," *Am. Soc. Rev. 5*, 13-27.

Osgood, C.E. (1969), "The Nature and Measurement of Meaning," in *Semantic Differential Technique, A Sourcebook*. Eds., J. G. Snider and C. Osgood. Chicago: Aldine Publ. Co.

Osgood, C.E., G.J. Suci, and P.H. Tannenbaum (1957), *The Measurement of Meaning*. Urbana: Univ. of Ill. Press.

Perlman, R. and R.L. Warren (1977), *Families in the Energy Crisis: Impacts and Implications for Theory and Policy*. Cambridge: Ballinger.

Phillips, K. (1978), "The Energy Battle: Why the White House Misfired," *Public Opinion, 1*, 9-14.

Rosenberg, M.J., C.I. Hovland, W.J. McGuire, R.P. Abelson, and J.W. Brehm (1960), *Attitude Organization and Change*. New Haven: Yale Univ. Press.

Roth, Julius A. (1965), "Hired Hand Research," *Amer. Soc., 1*, 190-196.

Schuman, H. and M.P. Johnson (1976), "Attitudes and Behavior," *Annual Review of Sociology, 2*. Palo Alto: Annual Reviews, 161-207.

Scott. R.A. and A. Shore (1974), "Sociology and Social Policy Analysis," *Amer. Soc. 9*, 51-59.

Scott, William A. (1968), "Attitude Measuremen," *Handbook of Social Psychology*, Vol. 2. Eds. G. Linzey and E. Aronson. Reading: Addison-Wesley.

Taylor, James B. (1961), "What Do Attitude Scales Measure: The Problem of Social Desirability," *J. Abnor. Soc. Psych., 62*, 386-390.

Thurstone, L.L. and E.J. Chave (1929), *The Measurement of Attitude*. Chicago: Univ. of Chi. Press.

Unseld, C.T. and R. Crews (1979), *Residential Solar Energy Users: A Review of Empirical Research and Related Literature*. SERI/TR-354-245. Golden: Solar Energy Research Institute, December.

Webb, Eugene J., Donald T. Campbell, Richard D. Schwartz, and Lee Sechrest (1966), *Unobtrusive Measures: Nonreactive Research in the Social Sciences*. Chicago: Rand McNally and Co.

Baruch Fischhoff, Paul Slovic,
Sarah Lichtenstein

3. Poorly Thought-out Values: Problems of Measurement

Abstract[1]

When faced with complex, unfamiliar issues, people may have poorly formulated, even incoherent, values. In such situations, where people do not know what they want, the values they express may be highly labile. Subtle changes in how issues are posed, questions are phrased, and responses are elicited can have marked effects on people's expressed preferences. Furthermore, confronting these effects is unavoidable if we are to elicit values at all. If one is interested in what an individual really feels about a value issue, there may be no substitute for an interactive elicitation procedure which acknowledges the elicitor's role in helping the repondent to create and enunciate values. There is, however, no guarantee that even the greatest of care will resolve fundamental inconsistencies in values.

Introduction

The elicitation of values lies at the heart of endeavors as varied as studying attitudes, buying a new car, and managing technological hazards. For example, almost all proposals for hazard management incorporate a division of labor between technical experts and the lay public, with the former responsible for the facts, the latter for the values. The experts know how things are (or at least can provide the best available guess), while the public knows how they should be. Such managerial schemes differ primarily in how these facts and values are to be combined and how the values are to be elicited. Some call for direct elicitation of values through surveys, hearings and the like, while others rely on the more indirect route of inferring values from the preferences "revealed" in market behavior. All share the assumption that people know what they want when it comes to the management of technologies.

Furthermore, although these opinions may not ordinarily be expressed in numerical (or even verbal) form, it is presumed that careful questioning can elicit a faithful representation of them. From this stance, interviewers see their elicitation procedures as neutral tools, bias-free channels which translate subjective feelings into analytically usable expressions. In no way do they impose the questioners' views on the respondents, beyond focusing attention on value issues that might otherwise be overlooked. Students of market behavior see life posing a series of problems that people resolve by exhibiting preferences that reflect their underlying values. In this light, life is an unending survey with real rather than hypothetical questions. It, too, presumably imposes no constraints on people's ability to express their true desires.

What happens, however, in cases where people do not know, or have difficulty appraising, what they want? Under such circumstances, elicitation procedures may become major forces in shaping the values expressed, or apparently expressed, in the responses they require. They can induce random error (by confusing the respondent), systematic error (by hinting at what the "correct" response is), or unduly extreme judgments (by suggesting clarity and coherence of opinion that are not warranted). In such cases, the method becomes the message. If elicited values are used to guide policy, they may lead to decisions not in the decision maker's best interest, to action when caution is desirable (or the opposite) to the obfuscation of poorly formulated views needing careful development and clarification.

The topic of this paper is the confrontation between those who hold (possiby inchoate) values and those who elicit values. By "values" we mean evaluative judgments regarding the relative or absolute worth or desirability of possible events, in short, the fundamental inputs to most conscious, deliberative decision making. Our only restriction is limiting the discussion to situations in which respondents are trying to report their values as honestly as possible; the further complications of measuring values in the face of strategic behavior are not considered. Although our argument is phrased in terms of questions posed by an interviewer, we see no fundamental difficulty with its extension to questions posed by the impersonal elicitor known as the market place.

The recurrent theme of this paper is that subtle aspects of how problems are posed, questions are phrased, and responses are elicited can have substantial impact on judgments that supposedly express people's true values. Furthermore, these issues are unavoidable: questions must be posed in some manner and that manner can have a large effect on the responses elicited. Pursuit of the issues raised here can alert elicitor and respondent to such impacts, making them deliberate rather than covert.

One might hope that such analysis would identify the *right* way to ask about values. To foreshadow our conclusions, we believe that the quest for a right way is, at times, ill-founded. Although there are some obvious pitfalls to avoid, incoherence is often inherent in our values. Rather than trying to circumvent lability, a better investment of effort might be to exploit the insight it provides into the nature of values and devise ways to live with uncertainty about what we want.

When and How People Might Not Know What They Want

People are most likely to have clear preferences regarding issues that are familiar, simple, and directly experienced. Each of these properties is associated with opportunities for trial-and-error learning, particularly such learning as may be summarized in readily applicable rules or homiles. Those rules provide stereotypic, easily justifiable responses to future questions of values. When adopted by individuals, they may be seen as habits; when adopted by groups, they constitute traditions.

The power of these rules of thumb comes from their development and application to simple and repetitive problems.[2] Their viability becomes suspect when the issues are unfamiliar and complex, the old intuitions impotent, the old rules untested and perhaps untestable. Unfortunately these are precisely the situations in which the elicitation of values is most important. Decision problems with high enough stakes and great enough complexity to justify investing in surveys or formal analysis are almost by definition unique and unfamiliar. They take us into situations for which we have never thought through the implications of the values and beliefs acquired in simpler settings. We may be unfamiliar with the terms in which issues are formulated (e.g., social discount rates, miniscule probabilities, or megadeaths). We may have contradictory values (e.g., a strong aversion to catastrophic losses of life and a realization that we're not more moved by a plane crash with 500 fatalities than one with 300). We may occupy different roles in life (parents, workers, children) which produce clear-cut, but inconsistent values. We may vacillate between incompatible, but strongly held, positions (e.g., freedom of speech is inviolate, but should be denied to authoritarian movements).

Table 1. Psychological States Associated with Not Knowing What You Want

- Having no opinion
  - Not realizing it
  - Realizing it
    - Living without one
    - Trying to form one
- Having an incoherent opinion
  - Not realizing it
  - Realizing it
    - Living with incoherence
    - Trying to form a coherent opinion
- Having a coherent opinion
  - Accessing it properly
  - Accessing only a part of it
  - Accessing something else

We may not even know how to begin thinking about some issues (e.g., the appropriate tradeoff between the opportunity to dye one's hair and a vague, minute increase in the probability of cancer 20 years from now). Our views may undergo changes over time (say, as the hour of decision approaches) and we may not know which view should form the basis of our decisions. Hypothetical considerations may be viewed quite differently when they become realities.

One possible partition of the psychological states that might accompany not knowing what we want appears in Table 1. Perhaps the most dangerous condition is the first, having no opinion and not realizing it. In that state, we may respond with the first thing that comes to mind once a question is asked and then commit ourselves to maintaining that first expression and to mustering support for it, while suppressing other views and uncertainties. As a result, we may be stuck with stereotypic or associative responses, generated without serious contemplation. Perhaps the most painful state is to acknowledge having incoherent or conflicting values that require resolution.

Psychophysics of Value

Many of the ways in which elicitation procedures can affect responses have been known since the beginnings of experimental psychology, over a century ago. Early psychologists concerned themselves with psychophysics, the study of the relationships between physical stimuli and the judgments expressed about them. They found that the threshold for discerning a stimulus and the threshold for discriminating between two stimuli depended on a variety of subtle features of how the stimuli were presented and how the response was elicited. Different judgments could be attached to the same stimuli as a function of whether those stimuli were presented in ascending (increasing on a physical continuum) or descending order, whether the set of stimuli was homogeneous or diverse, whether particular regions on the continuum were densely or sparsely represented, whether values near the threshold of detection were included or not, and whether the respondent made one or many judgments. Even when the same presentation was used, different judgments might be obtained with a numerical or a comparative (ordinal) response mode, with implicit instructions stressing speed or accuracy, with a bounded or an unbounded response set, and with verbal or numerical response labels.[3] As we shall see, such effects seem to be as endemic to judgments of value as they are to the judgmental context in which they were originally observed.

Inferring Values

Judgments are sensitive to these factors because the formulation of a response always involves an inferential process. In the context of values, when we are confronted with any interesting issue (for which habit or tradition do not dictate our answer), we must decide which of our basic values are relevant to that situation, how they are to be interpreted, and what weight each question is to be given (Rokeach, 1973). This process is governed in part by how the question is defined and in part by which perspectives we invoke in solving the inferential problem it poses. Once we have reached a summary judgment, we must decide how strongly we believe in it and in the perspectives upon which it is based. Finally, we must translate these opinions and impressions into a recordable response.

The next two sections describe how an elicitor can affect the formulation and expression of values by controlling the definition of problems, recruitment and integration of perspectives, and the confidence placed in the result of the inferential process. That control may be overt or covert, deliberate or inadvertent, reversible or irreversible. The succeeding section is devoted to the topic of irreversible effects, whereby the respondent is actually changed as a result of the elicitation process, through having existing perspectives destroyed or new ones created.

The notion of an external elicitor is used mainly as a syntactical device to avoid unclear antecedents. Questions of value must be posed in some way. If an external elicitor does not pose them for us, then we must pose them for ourselves (if only by accepting some "natural" formulation offered by our environment). Indeed, the power of the effects described here may be magnified when we pose problems to ourselves, unless we direct at our own question the same critical eye that we turn to someone else asking us about our values.

Defining the Issue

Is There a Problem?

Before a question of value can be posed, someone must decide that there is something to question. In this fundamental way, the elicitor impinges on the respondent's values. By asking about the desirability of premarital sex, interracial dating, daily prayer, freedom of expression, or the fall of capitalism, the elicitor may legitimate events that were previously viewed as unacceptable or cast doubts on events that were previously unquestioned. Opinion polls help set our national agenda by the questions they do and do not ask. Advertising helps set our personal agendas by the question it induces us to ask ourselves (two door or four door?) and those it takes for granted (more is better).

What Options and Consequences Are Relevant?

Once a question has been broached, its scope must be specified. Bounds must be placed on the options and consequences to be considered. The lore of survey research is replete with evidence regarding the subtle ways in which these bounds can be controlled by the elicitor's demeanor and the implicit assumptions and presumptions in the phrasing of questions (Payne, 1952; Rosenthal and Rosnow, 1969). There are, it seems, many ways to communicate to a respondent (a) whether the set of possible options is restricted to the named, the feasible, the popular, or the legal, (b) whether new options may be created, and (c) whether the question may be rejected out of hand. The set of relevant consequences may also be shaped to include or exclude intangible consequences (those without readily available dollar equivalents), ethical (versus efficiency) issues, social (versus personal) impacts, secondary and tertiary consequences, means (versus ends), and the well being of nature (versus that of humans). Control may be inadvertent as well as deliberate. For example, what may seem to the elicitor to be irrelevant and dominated alternatives, sensibly deleted for the sake of simplicity, may provide important contextual information for the respondent. Parducci (1974), for example, has found that judged satisfaction with one's state in life may depend highly on the range of possible states considered.

For the elicitor, a tempting solution would be to specify the problem as little as possible, allowing respondents to define the sets of options and consequences as they see fit. Unfortunately, this approach increases the probability that the elicitor and respondent will be talking about different things without solving the problem of inadvertent control Indeed, one might even argue that impassive elicitation is the most manipulative of all. For it means that the entire questioning experience is conducted under the influence of the unanalyzed predispositions and presumptions of the elicitor without even a courtesy warning to the respondent, "Here are my prejudices, let's try to be wary of them." There is no reason to believe that people will be spontaneously aware of what has been left out of the formulation (Tribe, 1972; Tribe et al., 1976; Fischhoff et al., 1978a).

How Should Options and Consequences Be Labeled?

The elicitor's influence on the definition of options and consequences does not end with their enumeration. Once the concepts have been evoked, they must be given labels. In a world with few hard evaluative standards, such symbolic interpretations may be very important (Marks, 1977). While the facts of abortion remain constant, individuals may vacillate in their attitudes as they attach and detach the label of "murder." The value of a dollar may change greatly if it is called "discretionary funds," "public funds," or "widows' and orphans' funds." The use of economic, psychological, or anthropocentric terminology may prejudge many problems.

Although not new, these issues are still troublesome. Furthermore, they cannot be avoided, for some meaning must be given to events, and the meaning generated by the respondent may be even less appropriate than that imposed by the elicitor (Poulton, 1977). When the respondent sees the validity of contradictory symbolic meanings (e.g., abortion both is and is not murder), the only recourse is to step back, somehow, and decide on exogenous grounds just what this elicitation session is all about. If necessary, that longer look should come sooner rather than later since changes in perspective are often irreversible (try to forget that "This is what I, your mother, want you to do, but decide for yourself") (Fischhoff, 1977).

How Should Values Be Measured?

After the problem has been structured, the units of measurement must be chosen. It is not difficult to construct options whose relative desirability is reversed when the evaluative criterion undergoes any of the following shifts: (a) from profit to regret, (b) from maximizing to satisficing, (c) from the fair price to the price I'd pay, (d) from final asset position to changes in asset position, (e) from the price I'd pay to avoid a malady to the price I'd have to be paid to accept it, (f) from lives saved to lives lost, and (g) from the ratio of benefits to costs to the difference between benefits and costs.[4] As before, choice of units may be specified by the elicitor or left to that nether region created by the "neutral" stance of non-specification.

Moreover, the size of the unit chosen may affect the responses. For example, unless some help is provided to the respondent (say, through the use of logarithmic scales), it may be very difficult to express values ranging over several orders of magnitude, simply because people find it hard to use either very small or very large numbers (Poulton, 1968).

Should the Problem be Decomposed?

Recognizing the subtlety and complexity of value issues, elicitors working within the context of procedures like decision analysis adopt a divide-and-conquer strategy (Keeney and Raiffa, 1976). Rather than risk having respondents fixate on a single aspect of a problem or treat all aspects superficially so as to minimize cognitive strain, these elicitors attempt to decompose the problem into manageable pieces.

Unfortunately, the act of decomposition may have consequences besides clarification. Divide-and-conquer strategies may destroy the respondent's intuitions. For example, if people think most naturally and adequately by analogy with past experiences, then all thought regarding issues of fact or value is context dependent (Dreyfus and Dreyfus, nd). Therefore, any attempt to evaluate the attributes of a particular event separately or to designate the importance of attributes in the abstract is likely to produce spurious results.

Another set of problems is raised by the fact that decompositions are not unique; different approaches may lead to different judgments of the same issue. Sequential evaluation of alternatives has been found to produce different preferences than simultaneous evaluation (Tversky, 1969). Plott and Levine (1978) have shown that the order in which attributes are considered is a crucial variable in determining preference orderings. Some theories of choice (Aschenbrenner, 1978) predict shifts in the attractiveness of simple gambles as a function of their decomposition. Kahneman and Tversky (1979) demonstrated a variety of reversals in preference depending on whether prospects were considered as a whole or decomposed into two stages.

Finally, as Tribe (1972) has argued, decomposition itself typically carries a message. It stresses ends over means. It proclaims the superiority of the elicitor's overall perspective and the overall social importance of analysis and its purveyors (Gouldner, 1976). It conveys a message of analyzability or solvability where that may be inappropriate.

Controlling the Respondent's Perspective

Altering the Accessibility of Perspectives

People solve problems, including the determination of their own values, with what comes to mind. The more detailed, exacting, and creative their inferential process is, the more likely they are to think of all they know about a question. The briefer that process becomes, the more they will be controlled by the relative accessibility of various considerations. Accessibility may be related to importance, but it is also related to degree of associative priming, the order in which questions are posed, imaginability, concreteness, and other factors only loosely related to importance.

One way in which the elicitor may unintentionally prime particular considerations is seen in Turner and Krauss' (1978) observation that people's confidence in national institutions was substantially higher in a National Opinion Research Center poll than in a contemporaneous Harris Poll which prefaced the confidence questions with six items relating to "political alienation." Another is the finding (Fischhoff et al., 1978a) that people judged the risks associated with various technologies to be more acceptable following a judgment task concerning the benefits of those technologies than following a task dwelling on their risks. According to Wildavsky (1966), the very act of asking people for their own personal values may suppress the availability of social values. Indeed, one could speculate that when conflicting values are relevant to a particular issue, the priming or evocation of one will tend to suppress the accessibility of its counterpart.

Expressed values sometimes reflect the direct application of established rules. Consistency with past preferences is one such rule; cautiousness is another. Whether or not a rule is evoked may depend upon situational cues. As an example of a rule that needed to be evoked before it was used, we have found that most people will prefer a gamble with a .25 chance to lose \$200 (and a .75 chance to lose nothing) to a *sure loss* of \$50. However, when that sure loss is called an *insurance premium,* people will reverse their preferences and forego the \$50. For these people, buying insurance was an acceptable but initially inaccessible rule; without a specific prompt, the sure loss was not seen as a premium.

Altering the Importance of Perspectives

Once an ensemble of relevant values has been elicited, some order must be placed on them. This ordering or weighting may also fall under elicitor control, with subtle, perhaps inadvertent, cues hinting at how much to think, what to look at and what responses are expected. For example, it is not hard to imagine the impact of an incredulous "hmm" or a querulous "half as important?" on the behavior of a confused or uncertain respondent. Nor is it hard to imagine how the demeanor of the elicitor might encourage or discourage the weight given to intangible values. Canavan-Gumpert (1977) has shown how reward and criticism can shift people's attention between the costs and benefits involved with a particular event.

One unavoidable decision made by the elicitor that may have great influence on the values that emerge is choice of response mode. Lichtenstein and Slovic (1973) showed that people use different cognitive processes when evaluating the worth of gambles via a comparative mode ("Which would you rather play?") than they use when judging each gamble separately ("How much is playing each worth to you?"). The different processes triggered by the change in response mode lead people to rather awkward reversals of preference ("I prefer A, but attach a higher value to B"). One possible explanation of such reversals (Slovic, 1975; Tversky, 1972) is that people make choices by searching for rules or concepts that provide a good justification, that minimize lingering doubts and that can be defended no matter what outcome occurs (e.g. "Quality is more important than quantity"). Different response modes may change the importance or salience of different rules. In the gambles example, A offered a higher probability of winning whereas B promised a greater payoff. Here, the preference mode may have emphasized that "the stakes don't matter if you're not going to win anyway," whereas the bidding mode focused attention on the payoff.

Another effect peculiar to choice behavior was found by Slovic and MacPhillamy (1974), who observed that dimensions common to each alternative had greater influence on choices than did dimensions that were unique to a particular alternative. Interrogation of the respondents after the study indicated that most did not intend to give more weight to the common dimension and were unaware that they had done so.

Choosing the Time of Inquiry

People's values change over time, sometimes systematically, sometimes not. The point in time at which the elicitor chooses to impinge on the respondent will partially determine what the respondent says. Some of these changes are fairly predictable. They include maturation, satiation, cumulative deprivation, increasing risk aversion as one approaches an event, and mood changes with time of day, day of the week, or season of the year. Consider people who regularly take stock of the world late at night and whose existential decisions are colored by their depleted body state. Are those values to be trusted or should one rely on the way they value their lives at high noon on a bright spring day? Should an elicitor rely on an auto worker's opinion of the intrinsic satisfaction of assembly-line work on the bus Monday morning or while on holiday and refreshed? In a 15-round experiment on insurance-buying behavior (Slovic et al., 1977), we found that participants who were generally risk seeking shifted to risk aversion on the final round (just before cashing out). Which attitude should we say characterized them? Or might not both of these perspectives be part of an individual's value system?

Any gap in time between judgment of an event and its occurrence may introduce an element of random or systematic variation in people's judgment. Hypothetical judgments of what an event would be like just may not capture how it will look in the flesh. Such failure of anticipation may lie behind the contrast between the limited funds budgeted for rescue operations and disaster relief and the almost unlimited resources made available for a particular rescue. We know relatively little about people's ability to anticipate the impact that future contingencies will have on their perceptions and values -- nor which perspective, the anticipated or the actual, is a better guide to action.

Altering Confidence in Expressed Values

The power of values comes from their role as guides to action. In that role, it may matter greatly what we believe their source to be, how strongly we believe in them and how coherent they seem. Attitudes towards values may, however, be as labile as the values themselves.

Much of the history of social psychology has involved identifying (or concocting) situations that lead people to adopt as their own, without critical analysis, values that originated with others (McGuire, 1969). One familiar way is through subtle pressures toward conformity. A second, less familiar way, involves arguing, even briefly, positions contrary to one's own. Misattribution may also occur when uncertainty leads respondents to look to others for cues as to what they want. Cognitive psychologists have recently offered some new wrinkles in the misattribution process, showing the ease with which presuppositions are absorbed as facts (Loftus et al., 1978), inferences are confused with direct observations (Harris and Monaco, 1978), and mere repetition improves the believability of statements (Hasher et al., 1977).

People will act and press others to act on the values in which they believe most deeply. Depth of belief is a function of source, as mentioned, and of the degree to which such values appear to be in conflict. A superficial analysis may create an illusion of confidence in values simply because conflicting values are not considered. Incoherence in beliefs is typically apparent only when the elicitor adopts or encourages different perspectives. It is easy to avoid taking that extra step, particularly when the respondent is interested in keeping things simple.

Such collusion toward simplicity is encouraged by one implicit message of many elicitation procedures: "This topic is knowable, analyzable; after one session, we will both know your values." It is magnified by the aura of precision and professionalism fostered by elaborate, numerical response modes. That aura manifests the can-do, technological-fix, mastery-of-the-world attitude that characterizes our society. Ellul (1969) has argued that one way to control people's minds is to lead them to believe that they can have an opinion on anything and everything. Those opinions will necessarily be superficial, guaranteeing that people will have elaborated, thoughtful positions on nothing. When we ask or answer questions of value, a useful antidote to overconfidence might be to recall the effort invested by Rawls (1971) and his colleagues to produce a reasonably coherent position on just one difficult issue, social justice.

Changing the Respondent

In most of the effects cited above, the elicitor neither creates nor destroys values, but merely affects the ways in which they are accessed, organized, and evaluated. Some, however, suggest ways in which the respondent may be irreversibly changed by the questioning procedure, perhaps for the better, perhaps for the worse. These fall into three generic categories. The elicitor may destroy an existing perspective on a value issue, create a perspective where none existed before, or deepen the respondent's understanding of the issue at hand or of value questions in general.

Destroying Existing Perspectives

As mentioned, one charge leveled against those who break complex questions of value into more manageable component questions is that their divide-and-conquer strategy destroys the intuitions of their respondents. A generalization of this position might be that any elicitation procedure deviating from the normal way in which judgments are made may erode the respondents' "feel" for the issue at hand. The failure of formal decision-making procedures to attract the loyalty of corporate decision makers has repeatedly been attributed to managers' refusal to trade the comforts of their intuitions for the promises of the formal methods (Harrison, 1977).

Other aspects of an elicitation mode may destroy parts of our "natural" perspective on issues. For example, the elicitor's efforts to maintain neutrality and to avoid influencing the respondent may deprive the respondent of the opportunity to observe others' values. Discussion with others may be a natural part of the way in which many people formulate their judgments. Such interaction may also be an effective procedure, perhaps by recruiting additional information and externalizing alternative perspectives that are too numerous to carry in one's head simultaneously. An elicitation procedure may be seen as destroying respondents' natural perspective whenever it deprives them of tools upon which they are accustomed to rely.

Creating Perspectives

An insidious possibility when posing unfamiliar questions to individuals with poorly formulated opinions is covertly creating a value where none existed. One possible process for accomplishing this feat is for the respondent to satisfy the elicitor's hunger for a recordable response by saying whatever comes to mind. Once emitted, this response may assume a life of its own. The respondent may subsequently conclude "If that's what I said, then that must be what I meant." Such positions can show a tenacity which is independent of their source of validity (Ross, 1977). The fact that such spontaneous responses are provided in a formal setting with a relatively esteemed listener may heighten such commitment effects, leading to newly invented, but firmly held, values. The very fact that one is out of one's depth in such situations makes it quite difficult to get a critical view on this new perspective.

Elicitation may induce people to think about issues they wish to avoid and would have ignored had they not been "bullied" by the elicitor. In some cases, the elicitor cannot be faulted for forcing people to take their heads out of the sand and face the issues implicit in the decisions they must make in any case. The use of decision analysis in medical contexts will create many such situations as physicians and patients are forced to provide explicit values for pain and death (Bunker et al., 1977) In other cases, the elicitor may be asking respondents to abrogate their own rights by telling, say, how much they would have to be compensated for a particular degradation to their environment without offering the response option "a clean environment is non-negotiable." In the extreme, the elicitor may be guilty of anaesthetizing moral feeling by inducing the respondent to think about the unthinkable. The mere act of thinking about some issues in cold, rational terms may lead to the legitimation of alternatives that should be dismissed outright.

Conclusion

An optimistic solution to the problems of lability is to claim that they can be handled by judicious use of sensitivity analysis. The decision maker thinks through the problem repeatedly, each time using different representatives from the distribution of possible values. If the final recommendation is insensitive to such changes, then the instability is considered to be inconsequential.

Whatever the promise of sensitivity analysis, in some contexts it completely misses the point. Many of the effects described here reflect the introduction of distorted perspectives or of newly created, possibly foreign, values into a decision-making process. Blanket invocation of sensitivity analysis will not excuse the imposition of an elicitor's perspective on the respondent. When shifts in perspective lead to reversals of preference, sensitivity analysis avoids the real issue of which response is, in fact, appropriate.

Elicitors must decide at some point whether or not they have adequately captured their respondents' values. The usual criteria are reliability and internal consistency (e.g., transitivity). However, where the task is poorly understood because of complexity or unfamiliarity, consistency of response within a given elicitation mode may tell us little beyond the power of that mode to impose a particular perspective. Consistency of response is a necessary but not sufficient condition for coherence of the underlying values. Greater insight into values may come from posing diverse questions in the hope of eliciting inconsistent responses. Therefore, one would want to start the study of values with methodological pluralism and treat inconsistency in expressed values as a success rather than a failure of measurement, for it indicates contexts defined sharply enough to produce a difference.

Although our discussion has emphasized unsavory aspects of the impact of the elicitor on the respondent, in the end, the only valid elicitation procedure may be a reactive one, designed to elaborate and deepen the respondent's perspective. Such interaction would represent a marked departure from the traditional model of the social scientist, impassively projecting stimuli against an objectified respondent. Rather, they would become colleagues exploring an issue together from the respondent's point of view.

How might the elicitor honestly affect the respondent's perspective, cultivating rather than distorting it? One reasonably safe way may be to help the respondent work through the logical implications of various points of view. A more difficult intervention is to educate respondents about the assumptions upon which their beliefs are contingent. Tougher still is trying to communicate factual information the respondent may not have known or taken into consideration. Although such deepening of perspective may be difficult, dangerous, and time consuming, an elicitor does small service to a respondent with incoherent values by asking questions that tap only a part of those values, particularly if that part might be abandoned (or endorsed more heartily) upon further contemplation.

In terms of Table 1, a carefully executed elicitation procedure should guarantee that if we have no opinion or an incoherent opinion, we will be forced to realize it. If our underlying values are coherent, we will accurately access them with a full understanding of their interrelations. However, no procedure can guarantee a polished product when the respondent starts with an incoherent opinion or none at all. One can hope that sensitive probing will reveal a reasonable procedure for weighting the various perspectives the respondent holds. It may even yield a reconceptualization of the problem through which apparent inconsistencies vanish.

In some cases though, the triangulation implicit in methodological pluralism will fail because there is no single coherent opinion in the respondent's mind waiting to be identified. Different perspectives will continue to evoke different opinions and they will not converge. Although more penetrating analyses are obviously called for in such circumstances, we must realize that values are shaped by experience as well as analysis. We may come to know what we want on complex environmental issues, for example, only by making decisions as best we can and waiting to see how well we like their consequences. Changes in attitudes toward the environment over the last decade must reflect at least in part the results of the expensive and intensive period of learning-by-doing following World War II. When we make these imperfect decisions, we will have to acknowledge explicitly the uncertainty surrounding our values, as well as that encumbering our factual knowledge. The result could be greater caution in our commitments or more deliberate experimentation designed to help us learn what we want.

Notes

[1]An earlier, expanded version of this paper appeared as Fischhoff et al. (1980). This work was supported by National Science Foundation under Grant PRA79-11934 to Clark University under subcontract to Perceptronics, Inc.

[2]However, one shouldn't tout folk or personal wisdom too highly. Even in those settings, people comfortably hold contradictory adages ("Nothing ventured, nothing gained" and "Fools rush in where wise men fear to tread"). The testing procedures for validating such wisdom leave much to be desired. People may not realize when experience provides a test for their well-worn rules and may not remember their experiences properly when they do consider validity. They may forget a rule's failures and remember its successes or vice versa. Finally, the translation of subjective feelings to observable judgments has an unavoidable error component due to inattention, distraction, laziness, and mistakes. Such error can introduce enough slippage into the opinion evaluation and formulation process to make clarity somewhat difficult.

[3]No attempt will be made to document this incomplete list drawn from various parts of the lore of psychology. Useful references include Carterette (1974) and Kling and Riggs (1971).

[4]Kahnman and Tversky (1979) provide the most extensive and insightful discussion of the power of shifts in point of reference, the principle underlying most of these effects.

References

Aschenbrenner, K. M. (1978), "Single-peaked Risk Preferences and Their Dependability on the Gambles' Presentation Mode," *J. Exp. Psych*: *Human Perception and Performance, 4,* 513-520.

Bunker, J. P., B. A. Barnes, and F. Mosteller (1977). *Costs, Risks and Benefits of Surgery.* New York: Oxford.

Canavan-Gumpert, D. (1977), "Generating Reward and Cost Orientation Through Praise and Criticism," *J. Per. Soc. Psych., 35,* 501-513.

Carterette, E. C. and M. P. Friedman (Eds.) (1974), *Handbook of Perception, Vol. II.* New York: Academic Press.

Dreyfus, H., and S. Dreyfus (nd), "Uses and Abuses of Multiattribute and Multiaspect Models of Decision Making," U.C. Berkeley, unpublished manuscript.

Ellul, J. (1969). *Propaganda.* New York: Knopf.

Fischhoff, B. (1977), "Perceived Informativeness of Facts," *J. Exp. Psych.*: *Human Perception and Performance, 3,* 349-358.

Fischhoff, B., P. Slovic, S. Lichtenstein, S. Read, and B. Combs (1978a), "How Safe is Safe Enough? A Psychometric Study of Attitudes Toward Technological Risks and Benefits," *Policy Science, 8,* 127-152.

Fischhoff, B., P. Slovic, and S. Lichtenstein (1978b), "Fault Trees: Sensitivity of Estimated Failure Probabilities to Problem Representation," *J. Exp. Psych.*: *Human Perception and Performance, 4,* 342-255.

Fischhoff, B., P. Slovic, and S. Lichtenstein (1980), "Knowing What You Want: Measuring Labile Values," in T. Wallsten (Ed.), *Cognitive Processes in Choice and Decision Behavior.* Hillsdale, NJ: Erlbaum.

Gouldner, A. (1976). *The Dialectic of Ideology and Technology*: *The Origins, Grammar, and Future of Ideology.* New York: Seabury Press.

Grether, D. M. and C. R. Plott (1979), "Economic Theory of Choice and Preference Reversal Phenomenon," *American Economic Review, 69,* 623-638.

Harris, R. J. and R. E. Monaco (1978), "Psychology of Pragmatic Implications: Information Processing Between the Lines," *J. Exp. Psych: Gen., 107,* 1-22.

Harrison, F. L. (1977), "Decision Making in Conditions of Extreme Uncertainty," *J. Mgmt. Studies, 14,* 169-178.

Hasher, L., D. Goldstein, and T. Toppino (1977), "Frequency and the Conference of Referential Validity," *J. Verbal Learning and Verbal Behavior, 16,* 107-110.

Kahneman, D. and A. Tversky (1979), "Prospect Theory," *Econometrica, 47,* 263-292.

Keeney, R. L. and H. Raiffa (1976). *Decisions with Multiple Objectives.* New York: Wiley.

Kling, J. and L. Riggs (1971). *Woodworth and Schlosberg's Experimental Psychology.* New York: Holt, Reinhart, Winston.

Lichtenstein, S. and P. Slovic (1973), "Response-induced Reversals of Preference in Gambling: An Extended Replication in Las Vegas," *J. Exp. Psych., 101,* 16-20.

Loftus, E., D. O. Miller, and H. J. Burns (1978), "Semantic Integration of Verbal Information into Visual Memory," *J. Exp. Psych.: Human Learning and Memory, 4,* 19-31.

Marks, B. A. (1977), "Decision under Uncertainty: The Narrative Sense," *Administration and Society, 9,* 379-394.

McGuire, W. J. (1969), "The Nature of Attitudes and Attitude Change," *The Handbook of Social Psychology.* (Eds.) G. Lindzey and E. Aronson, Reading, MA: Addison-Wesley.

Parducci, A. (1974), "Contextual Effects: A Range-Frequency Analysis," *Handbook of Perception Vol. II.* (Eds.) E. C. Carterette and M. P. Friedman, New York: Academic Press.

Payne, S. L. (1952). *The Art of Asking Questions.* Princeton: Princeton University Press.

Plott, C. R. and M. E. Levine (1978), "A Model of Agenda Influence on Committee Decisions," *American Economic Review, 68,* 146-160.

Poulton, E. C. (1968), "The New Psychophysics: Six Models for Magnitude Estimation," *Psychological Bulletin, 69,* 1-19.

Poulton, E. C. (1977), "Quantitative Subjective Assessments Are Almost Always Biased, Sometimes Completely Misleading," *British Journal of Psychology, 68,* 409-425.

Rawls, J. (1971). *A Theory of Justice.* Cambridge: Harvard University Press.

Rokeach, M. (1973). *The Nature of Human Values.* New York: The Free Press.

Rosenthal, R. and R. L. Rosnow (1969). *Artifact in Behavioral Research.* New York: Academic Press.

Ross, L. (1977), "The Intuitive Psychologist and His Shortcomings," *Advances in Social Psychology.* (Ed.) L. Berkowitz, New York: Academic Press.

Slovic, P. and D. J. MacPhillamy (1974), "Dimensional Commensurability and Cue Utilization in Comparative Judgement," *Organizational Behavior and Human Performance, 11,* 172-194.

Slovic, P. (1975), "Choice Between Equally-valued Alternatives," *J. Exp. Psych.: Human Perception and Performance, 1,* 80-287.

Slovic, P., B. Fischhoff, S. Lichtenstein, B. Corrigan, and B. Combs (1977), "Preference for Insuring Against Probable Small Losses: Implications for the Theory and Practice of Insurance," *J. of Risk and Insurance, 44,* 237-258.

Tribe, L. H. (1972), "Policy Science: Analysis or Ideology?" *Philosophy and Public Affairs, 2,* 66-110.

Tribe, L. H., L. S. Schelling, and J. Voss (1976). *When Values Conflict: Essays on Environmental Analysis, Discourses and Decision.* Cambridge, MA: Ballinger Publishing Co.

Turner, C. F. and E. Krauss (1978), "Fallible Indicators of the Subjective State of the Nation," *American Psychologist, 33,* 456-470.

Tversky, A. (1972), "Elimination by Aspects: A Theory of Choice," *Psychological Review, 79,* 281-299.

Tversky, A. (1969), "Intransitivity of Preferences," *Psychological Review, 76,* 31-48.

Wildavsky, A. (1966), "The Political Economy of Efficiency: Cost-Benefit Analysis, Systems Analysis and Program Budgeting," *Public Administration Review, 26,* 292-308.

Jon D. Miller

4. A Conceptual Framework for Understanding Public Attitudes Toward Conservation and Energy Issues

Abstract

This chapter sets attitudes toward conservation and energy issues in the broader context of issue specialization and outlines an attentive public model to interpret available empirical public attitude data. The discussion focuses on several of the studies to be included in the empirical section as well as some collaborating data from a recent NSF-sponsored survey of adults in the United States.

Introduction

A review of the literature concerning public attitudes toward materials conservation, energy, and related scientific issues reveals a growing volume of surveys generated by persons and groups with a strong interest in the substantive questions involved, but largely uninformed by current social science theory concerning attitude formation. The purpose of this chapter is to outline a stratified model of public attitudes toward low-saliency topics like materials conservation and energy policy issues.

As a starting point, it is necessary to differentiate among opinions, attitudes, and belief systems. Hennessy (1972) has provided a useful set of distinctions, suggesting that opinions are lightly held reactions to non- salient stimuli and are usually unorganized and subject to easy change. Attitudes are more organized and strongly held views of salient issues. Attitudes are usually stable and are often the basis for specific behaviors -- like voting or contacting an official. Belief systems are totally structured and organized sets of attitudes -- like Marxism, liberalism, or conservatism.

This discussion will focus on attitudes toward materials conservation and energy policy issues. Opinions are too ephemeral and have no impact on the political system and policy outcomes. Belief systems are interesting, but too rare to be helpful in understanding actual policy outcomes.

Utilizing opinions and attitudes as defined above, it is important to distinguish between consumer behaviors and policy attitudes. A portion of the relevant literature focuses on consumer preferences and behaviors concerning the packaging and use of various products. When survey researchers ask consumers about rarely used products or hypothetical situations, most often they are tapping consumer opinions which are unstable and unreliable. When consumers are queried about preferences for and consumption of products that they use regularly and which are important to them, then it is likely that basic and continuing attitudes are measured. In general, it is reasonable to expect that most adults have some consumer attitudes relevant to materials and energy conservation.

In contrast, it is unlikely that most adults have any policy attitudes toward materials and energy conservation issues. While consumer attitudes are generally based on concrete experiences, policy attitudes are markedly more abstract and outside the personal experience of the vast majority of Americans. National cross-sectional surveys concerning issues related to materials and energy conservation policy will tap mainly unstable attitudes and will be of limited value. This situation is not unique to materials conservation, energy, or related scientific issues, but rather reflects an attitude structure common to a wide array of low-saliency issues. It is useful to turn to the general case first, and then return later to assess the import of the general model on this specific substantive area.

The Problem of Saliency

A low level of public interest and information is not unique to attitudes toward energy or materials conservation. At this point, the broader social science literature becomes especially helpful. For any given person, the range of possible areas of interest is vast. One of the characteristics of modern society is that the volume of information is overwhelming, and no single individual can become knowledgeable or remain current in more than a relatively narrow range of topics. Ironically, many groups of persons with an intense interest in an area tend to think that everyone ought to be knowledgeable about that particular area. The public apathy toward agricultural policy, foreign policy, the problems of the aged, prison record, national health insurance, endangered species, environmental quality, and modern child-raising theory is decried regularly.

The low level of public understanding of science and technology is not fundamentally different from the low levels of public understanding of a number of other public issues. Only a small proportion of the adult population follows foreign policy developments among the nations of the world and a smaller proportion yet understands the symbolic exchange of words and actions that leads to the formulation of foreign policy in the twentieth century. Gabriel Almond published in 1950 an analysis of attitudes toward foreign policy in his *The American People and Foreign Policy*. In this work, Almond argued that the great majority of the adult population was uninterested in foreign policy matters, becoming interested only in times of war and the activation of the military draft. Most of the time, the public monitoring of foreign policy is conducted by a much smaller portion of the population, which Almond termed the "attentive public." This attentive public is generally better educated, has more income, and holds more prestigious employment than the general population (see Figure 1). The basic model is useful in a number of substantive areas.

Almond suggests that an attentive public is largely a self-selected group, and that it communicates through specialized channels. Many of the members of the attentive public tend to be members of voluntary groups and associations of academic and professional organizations with strong interests in a given issue area. Rosenau (1961, 1963) and others (Hero, 1959, 1960; Cohen, 1973; and Mueller, 1973) have provided a substantial empirical description of the attentive public for foreign policy. Two recent studies have profiled the attentive public for science policy (Miller, Suchner, Voelker, 1980; Miller, Prewitt, Pearson, 1980).

Generally, the issues are formulated for an attentive public by a still smaller group of policy specialists, who are non-governmental spokesmen for various points of view. Almond labels this group "policy elites." These specialists may include corporate or labor leaders, academic leaders, or editors of some of the specialized communications media. They debate among themselves and thus help to keep the attentive public informed about the problems and alternatives in given policy areas. They also interact with the top of the pyramid, the decision-makers.

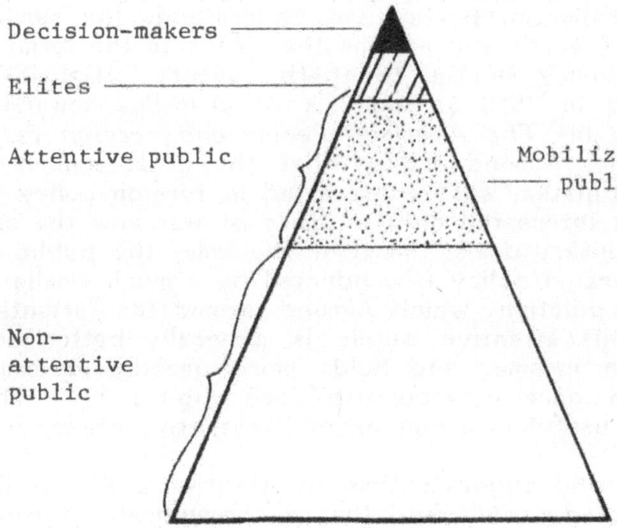

Figure 1. The Almond Model.

Rosenau (1974) has divided the attentive public into a "mobilized public" and a non-mobilized segment. The mobilized public goes beyond interest and information acquisition and seeks to influence policy through overt actions. It is this mobilized group that writes legislators and executives, testifies at hearings, and privately lobbies decision-makers to secure desired policy outcomes.

At the top of Almond's public opinion pyramid sit the decision-makers. Decision- makers have the power to make binding decisions in a given policy area. In contrast, policy elites may only recommend or urge a given policy decision.

The Attentive Public for Energy Policy

In view of the utility of the Almond model for understanding a wide range of low-saliency topics, it is appropriate to turn to the process of adapting the model to those issues concerning energy policy. As a first step, it will be helpful to conceptualize the probable membership of each of the strata in the basic model. The decision-makers for energy policy would include the President and his principal advisors and cabinet officers dealing with energy-related topics; the leadership of the Congress, and especially the committee leadership of energy-relevant committees in the House and Senate; the leadership of major scientific research centers and corporate energy enterprises; and, occasionally, judicial officers, state officers, and local officials (Rettig, 1977; Jachim, 1975; Greenberg, 1967).

Policy leaders in the energy area are numerous and reflect the decentralized nature of both scientific research and the utility industry in the United States. These leaders are active in formulating policy alternatives and advocating particular solutions or programs. They include the leaders of scientific societies, the directors of major research centers and laboratories, the top management of energy corporations, editors and writers, and self-selected public interest advocates (Zuckerman,1977; Mulkay,1976; Whitley,1976; Nelkin, 1977). For this latter group, self-selected is not meant in a derogatory sense, but rather to denote persons who develop an interest in energy issues, become knowledgeable, and exert influence and leadership among the attentive public.

The attentive public for energy policy would include those persons who choose to inform themselves on energy issues and topics and to follow the debate of issues. While a more formal operational definition will be offered below, the attentive public for energy might be expected to include a significant number of practicing scientists, energy-related businessmen, clergy, and citizens concerned about one or more specific issues related to energy. The attentive public for energy would not be very large, but its size might be expected to increase as the educational level of the populace continues to increase.

For the most part, the mass public would be expected to hold few structured attitudes toward energy policy issues. Following Converse (1964), the mass public would display little energy policy information if open-ended questions were utilized. At the same time, it should be noted that special topics can generate short-term interest, and the mass public may become politically active on a given topic. The bitter local fights over fluoridations that punctuated the 1950's and the early 1960's are an excellent example (Mausner and Mausner, 1955; Kirscht and Knutson,1961; Davis,1960; Gamson, 1966). The siting of nuclear power plants has generated similar local disputes in numerous communities (Nelkin,1971,1974; Richardson,1974; Carter,1976; Doderlein,1976). There is little evidence that these flashes of interest have had any long-term impact and that any significant number of persons move into the attentive public for energy policy as a result of these single-issue fights.

The Definition and Measurement of Attentiveness

In his original discussion of attentiveness, Almond (1950) defined members of an attentive public to be those individuals who (1) displayed a high level of interest in a topic, (2) possessed an adequate level of current information on the subject, and (3) were committed to a pattern of information acquisition that would assure a continuing level of knowledgeability.

Following Almond, this analysis treats attentiveness as the combination of all three of these attributes, not just one or two of them. For example, a person who had taken some science courses in college might have the minimal information level necessary to qualify on that dimension, but not be particularly interested in energy policy issues and not committed to a regular pattern of information acquistion. In a similar vein, immediately after an incident such as the Three Mile Island accident, it would have been possible to find a number of people who had a high level of interest in at least some energy policy issues and who had been able to acquire enough current information from the general media to meet a reasonable test of knowledgeability but who were not regular information consumers and who might be expected to experience a decline in both interest and information as time passed from the point of stimulus. While this is an intersting and important group to study and understand, they do not constitute the attentive public in our sense because their involvement is likely to be short-term in the absence of a pattern of regular information acquisition related to energy policy issues.

In 1979, the National Science Foundation commissioned a survey of public attitudes toward science and technology that included a significant number of items concerning energy policy issues.[1] The survey was a multi-stage national cluster sample of 1635 adults, aged 17 and over. These data allow the construction of measures of the three components of the attentiveness to energy policy issues.

The level of respondent interest in energy policy issues was measured by a direct inquiry. Each respondent was presented with a card listing nine public policy areas and was asked to report for each whether he was very interested, moderately interested, or not at all interested. One of the nine issue areas was "issues about energy policy," and 47 percent of the respondents reported a high level of interest (see Table 1). A high level of interest in energy policy issues was positively associated with higher levels of formal education, professional and managerial employment, higher socio-economic status, and the male gender.

Using the same list of issue areas, each respondent was asked to classify himself as very well informed, moderately informed, or poorly informed about each of the nine issue areas. Approximately three-quarters of the adult population classified themselves as very well or moderately well informed about energy policy issues (see Table 1). The demographic distribution of energy policy information follows the general outline of interest in energy issues.

The third dimension of the attentiveness typology is a regular pattern of relevant information acquisition. As discussed above, it is important to have some indication of a continuing interest in a given issue area for a respondent to be classified as attentive to a given substantive area. The information acquisition dimension was conceptualized to include the regular consumption of both general political news and specialized scientific or energy-relevant information. Two separate indices were constructed to represent these two facets of information consumption. The Index of General News Consumption included watching television news daily, watching television documentaries frequently, listen-

Table 1. Public Interest In, Knowledge About, and Attentiveness to Energy Policy Issues.

	High Interest	High Know-ledge	Acqui-sition	Regular Energy Attentive	N
All Adults	47	76	47	25	1635
Gender					
Female	42	73	41	20	862
Male	53	80	53	31	773
Age					
17-24	38	64	35	16	309
25-34	49	84	57	31	361
35-44	48	76	45	27	258
45-54	57	80	54	29	234
55-64	49	78	52	30	228
65 and over	41	63	37	18	245
Education					
LT high school	40	62	25	12	465
High school	44	78	42	21	550
Some college	50	81	60	33	382
Baccalaureate	56	93	76	44	146
Graduate degree	67	93	82	54	92
Occupation					
Prof & Tech	54	85	70	38	258
Managerial	54	82	59	35	170
Sales	54	79	61	36	90
Clerical	46	80	45	25	283
Craftsman	52	79	47	28	168
Operative	41	68	33	15	235
Laborer	38	71	42	15	64
Farm Worker	32	66	28	12	32
Service Worker	42	72	30	18	187
Respondent SES					
Low	40	63	28	15	339
Medium	48	80	46	25	728
High	58	90	76	46	298

ing to the radio news often, reading a daily newspaper, or reading a weekly news magazine (up to three were counted). The Index ranged from zero to seven. The Index of Specialized News Consumption included watching the Ascent of Man television series, watching National Geographic specials, visiting a science or natural science museum, watching the Nova television series, reading a general science magazine (up to three counted), or reading a scientific or energy-relevant professional journal (up to three counted).The Index ranged from zero to 11, but no single respondent scored more than six on the index.

To provide a single summary measure of information acquisition, the general and specialized news consumption indices were combined into a dichotomous typology of information acquisition. To be classified as a regular consumer of scientific or energy-relevant information, a respondent needed to:

(1) consume one or two general news sources and two or more specialized science or energy-related news sources, or

(2) consume three or more general information sources and at least one specialized information source.

Using this typology of information acquisition, the 1979 survey data indicate that 47 percent of the adult population are regular consumers of scientific or energy-relevant information (see Table 1). As with the other dimensions of attentiveness, a regular pattern of information acquisition is positively associated with higher levels of formal education and with the male gender.

To qualify as attentive to energy policy, a respondent had to score high on all three dimensions of the typology -- interest, knowledge, and information acquisition. When these three dimensions are combined, the data from the 1979 survey indicate that 25 percent of the adult population of the United States are attentive to energy policy issues. Energy attentiveness is positively and strongly associated with higher levels of formal education, higher socio-economic status, and the male gender (see Table 1).

Given the prominence of energy issues in the mass media in recent years and the personalization of energy issues in the form of higher prices and periodic scarcity, it is perhaps surprising that the level of attentiveness is not greater. At the same time, it is important to re-emphasize the difference between attentiveness and concern about an issue. Given energy prices and gas lines, it is clear that more than a quarter of the adult population have some con-

Table 2. Percentage of Energy Policy Attentives Who Report High Interest and Knowledge About Other Issues.

	Percent
Local school issues	23
Foreign policy	34
Agricultural issues	25
Scientific issues	54
Economic and business issues	45
Minority rights	24
New inventions and technologies	53
Womens rights	22
N = 412	

cern about energy issues, but these data suggest that for many persons this concern is not expressed in policy terms. There is a substantial literature that suggests that most adults do not think in policy terms (Converse, 1964) and these data confirm previous findings in this regard. In contrast, attentives do tend to think in policy terms and are more likely to be able to evaluate policy level decisions by the government and policy recommendations by various contending interest groups. Further, it is the attentive public that is most likely to contact decision-makers and to seek to influence the formulation of energy policy.

At this point, it is useful to turn our attention to three remaining questions. First, does attentiveness to energy policy issues constitute a reasonably distinct cluster of policy interests? Second, does the attentive public for energy issues have policy views that differ from non-attentives? Third, what are the implications of this model for understanding public attitudes toward materials conservation and energy policy issues?

Energy Attentiveness in the Context of Other Issues

Since a number of other attentive publics have already been identified and profiled, it is reasonable to ask if the attentive public for energy policy is in fact a reflection of attentiveness to other issues (i.e., scientific, technologic, or economic issues) or if it is a reasonably distinct cluster of policy interests. Further, it is useful to ask if the attentive public for energy policy is fundamentally an elitist or pluralist phenomenon.

To set attentiveness to energy policy in a broader context, it is useful to examine the other areas of interest and information of those respondents classified as energy attentives. Using the data from the 1979 survey, it was possible to calculate the percentage of energy attentives who reported a high level of interest in and a moderate to high level of knowledge about eight other issue areas. An examination of the results indicates that about half of those persons attentive to energy policy issues are also attentive to scientific, technologic, or economic issues, but that the levels of interest in other issues are significantly lower (see Table 2).

The positive association with science and technology attentiveness is not surprising since numerous facets of energy policy involve scientific and technological judgements. To the contrary, a significantly lower level of association

Table 3. Differences in Attitudes and Knowledge Between Energy Attentives and Nonattentives

	Attentives	Nonattentives
Percent declaring that the benefits of scientific research strongly outweigh the harmful results.	61%	41%
Percent scoring high on the Index of Expectations of Science.	40	22
Percent reporting a clear understanding of "radiation".	65	43
Percent reporting a clear understanding of "GNP".	53	23
Percent in favor of siting a nuclear power plant in their area.	38	27
Percent that would definitely take an active role in a local dispute over the siting of a nuclear power plant.	39	19
Percent scoring high on the Index of Political Activity.	44	19
N =	412	1223

Note: All of the differences reported in this table are significant at the .05 level.

would have been more difficult to understand. But the fact that only half of the energy attentives also held a comparable interest in science and technology indicates that approximately half of the energy attentives approach the issues from other perspectives.

Further, the distribution of joint areas of interest, ranging from minority rights to agricultural policy, demonstrates the pluralistic nature of the attentiveness process. If the data had shown no relationship at all between energy attentiveness and agricultural policy, for example, the results would have suggested an outcome at odds with the known parameters of issue interest in the American political system. These data indicate that energy issues are very much a part of the fabric of American politics in the latter part of the 20th century.

The Policy Views of Energy Attentives and Nonattentives

The second important issue to address is the distinctiveness of the policy views of the attentive public for energy issues. If the views of the attentive public do not differ from the views of non-attentives, then there is little analytic or substantive value in knowing which persons are attentive and which are not. Fortunately, the 1979 survey of adult attitudes toward science and technology included a number of items pertaining to energy policy issues and it is possible to contrast the views and knowledge base of the two groups.

First, in regard to general views of science and technology, the 1979 data indicate that persons attentive to energy policy issues are significantly more likely to hold positive views of the present risk-benefit ratio of scientific research and to have higher expectations for future scientific research. Slightly over 60 percent of the attentive public for energy policy issues assert that the benefits of scientific research "strongly outweigh" the harmful results in contrast to only 41 percent of non-attentives. Similarly, 40 percent of energy attentives score high on an Index of Expectations of Science in contrast to 22 percent of non-attentives (see Table 3).

Second, in regard to some of the basic terms used in the discussion of energy issues, the data from the 1979 survey indicate that attentives are significantly more likely to understand terms like "radiation" or "GNP" than are non-attentives. The significant difference on these items confirms the self-reported levels of issue information used in the construction of the original attentiveness typology.

Third, on the issue of the use and siting of nuclear power plants, the 1979 data indicate that energy attentives are more favorable to nuclear power than nonattentives, and much more likely to take an active part in a local dispute on a siting issue. It should be noted that the question concerns the location of a nuclear power plant in the area where the respondent lives, and is not a general policy question about the use of nuclear power at other locations or in general. As confirmation of the participation finding, the data also indicate that energy attentives are more likely to be active in general political events than are persons not attentive to energy issues (see Table 3).

Looking at the differences, it is clear that the policy views and the policy relevant information base of energy attentives and nonattentives differ significantly. Without passing judgment about the desirability of the direction of the views of the attentives, it is clear that persons wishing to influence the energy policy process ought to be aware of the dispositions of the attentive public for energy policy.

Implications for Materials Conservation and Energy Policy Research

The basic purpose of this chapter has been the introduction of a conceptual model for approaching the study of attitudes toward materials conservation and energy policy issues. In the preceding sections, the attitude development literature was reviewed and a stratified model of selective attentiveness was introduced, operationalized, and analyzed. At this point, it is important to turn to the policy implications of the selective attentiveness model for the present and future study of attitudes toward materials conservation and energy policy. Four major implications appear worthy of discussion.

First, the discussion of the literature and the brief review of some of the data on policy thinking would argue strongly for separating the problem of consumer behavior and the problem of policy attitudes. As demonstrated in the discussion and analysis above, policy thinking is relatively rare in the American public. The relevant attentive public includes only a quarter of the total public. In contrast, consumer behavior problems include a vast portion of the population and involve a fundamentally different dynamic.

Second, the identification of an attentive public for energy policy issues suggests that one should be cautious of mass public attitude surveys. While the works of Melber and of Clelland and Bremseth that follow are interesting and useful in many respects, it is important for the reader to understand that most members of the mass public do not have attitudes on materials conservation and energy matters in Hennessy's sense and that many of the opinions on these issues are fragile. An understanding of the selective attentiveness process can help the reader interpret some of the results of mass surveys more usefully. In the report by Clelland and Bremseth, for example, they find that the opponents of the breeder reactor are more active and better informed than its supporters, but this finding may be seen as reflecting the likelihood that nearly all of the opponents are members of the attentive public for energy issues whereas the remainder of the survey respondents would include a large number of nonattentives who were not aware of the issue. It may be that a majority of the attentive public for energy would support a breeder program, but the mixing of attentives and nonattentives in a mass sample makes that determination most difficult.

Third, it is important to conceptualize the attentive public as the linkage between the public and the decision makers. Since most of the mass public is not attentive, the attentive public becomes a surrogate public and plays much the same role often visualized for the public at large in pure democratic theory. The attentive public listens to the debate of the issues, digests the arguments and the data, and then participates in the political process -- electoral and non-electoral -- to translate its feelings into public policy. In studies like the one reported by Otway later in this volume, the author contrasts the views of decision-makers and the general public, but the study fails to include a linkage group like the attentive public. Had the Otway study been conceptualized as a stratified model or were future studies of this type to utilize the selective attentiveness model, it would be possible to examine the transmission process of attentive attitudes and preferences through non-governmental leadership groups and individuals and to the decision-makers. This is not to fault the many very useful contribtions of Otway's work, but to suggest another view of the work from the vantage point of the conceptual model outlined in this chapter.

Finally, for persons interested in influencing public policy toward materials conservation and energy policies, the model suggested herein provides some relatively specific practical guidance. Policy changes in this area will not be achieved through mass political involvement, but rather through the activation of the attentive publics involved in the issues. These groups are smaller in number, more homogeneous in character, and relatively easier to locate than the mass public. The attentive public for energy policy acquires its information from a relatively limited number of specialized information channels and it is less difficult and less expensive to gain access to these channels than a comparable mass public information campaign. At the same time, it should be recognized that the members of the attentive public for energy are persons who are basically comfortable with the risk-benefit ratio approach to thinking about issues and they are not easily persuaded of policy conclusions.

In summary, it is clear that the American political system will face a number of important issues in the years and decades ahead involving both materials conservation and energy policy in general. Most of these issues will be decided outside the electoral arena through legislature committees and executive branch administrative decisions. The processes by which these issues are debated and ultimately decided deeply involve that segment of society that we have described as the attentive public for energy policy. The concept has considerable promise both for understanding the present disposition of materials conservation and energy policy issues and for developing strategies for the future resolution of these issues.

Notes

[1]The survey and interview schedule were designed by Jon D. Miller and Kenneth Prewitt under NSF contract SRS78-16839. The data were collected by the Institute for Survey Research at Temple University under contract SRS79-25118. The data were analyzed by Miller, Prewitt, and Pearson (1980) under NSF contract SRS78-16839. All interpretations of the data reported herein are those of the author and do not necessarily reflect the views of the National Science Foundation.

References

Almond, G.A. (1950), *The American People and Foreign Policy*. New York: Harcourt, Brace, and Co.

Carter, L.J. (1976), "Nuclear Initiatives: Two sides Disagree on Meaning of Defeat," *Science 194*, 811-12.

Cohen, B.C. (1959), *The Influence of Non-Governmental Groups in Foreign Policy-Making*. Boston: World Peace Foundation.

Cohen, B.C. (1973), *The Public's Impact on Foreign Policy*. Boston: Little, Brown, and Co.

Converse, P. (1964), "The Nature of Belief systems in Mass Publics." *Ideology and Discontent*, D.E. Apter, ed. New York: Free Press.

Davis, M. (1960), "Community Attitudes Toward Fluoridation," *Public Opinion Quarterly 23*, 74-82.

Doderlien, J.M. (1976), "Nuclear Power, Public Interest and the Professional," *Nature 264*, 202-203.

Gamson, W.A. (1968), "Rancorous Conflict in Community Politics," *American Sociological Review 32*, 71-81.

Greenberg, D. (1967), *The Politics of Pure Science*. New York: Plume.

Hennessy, B. (1972), *Political Attitudes and Public Opinion*. D.D. Nimmo and C.M. Bonjean, Eds. New York: McKay.

Hero, A.O. (1959), *Americans in World Affairs*. Boston: World Peace Foundation.

Hero, A.O. (1960), *Voluntary Organizations in World Affairs*. Boston: World Peace Foundation.

Jachim, A.G. (1975), *Science Policy Making in the United States: The Batavia Accelerator*. Carbondale: Southern Illinois University Press.

Kirscht, J.P. and A.A. Knutson (1961), "Science and Fluoridation: An Attitude Study," *Journal of Social Issues 17*, 37-44.

Mausner, B. and J. Mausner (1955), "A Study of the Anti-Scientific Attitude," *Scientific American 192*, 35-39.

Miller, J.D.; K. Prewitt and R. Pearson (1980), *The Attitudes of the U.S. Public Toward Science and Technology*. A final report to the National Science Foundation.

Miller, J.D., R.W. Suchner, and A.V. Voelker (1980), *Citizenship in an Age of Science*. New York: Pergamon.

Mueller, J.E. (1973), *War, Presidents and Public Opinion*. New York: John Wiley and Sons.

Mulkay, M. (1976), "The Mediating Role of the Scientific Elite," *Social Studies of Science 6*, 445.

Nelkin, D. (1974), "Threats and Promises: Negotiating the Control of Research." The Role of Experts in a Nuclear Siting Controversy. *Bulletin of the Atomic Scientists, 30, 9*, 29-36.

Nelkin, D. (1971), *Nuclear Power and Its Critics*. Ithaca: Cornell University Press.

Nelkin, D. (1977), *Technical Decisions and Democracy*. Beverly Hills, Ca.: Sage Publications.

Rettig, R.A. (1977), *Cancer Crusade: The Story of the National Cancer Act of 1971*. Princeton, N.J.: Princeton University Press.

Richardson, R.A. (1974), "The Selling of the Atom," *Bulletin of the Atomic Scientists, 30:8*, 28-35.

Rosenau, J. (1974), *Citizenship Between Elections*. New York: Free Press.

Rosenau, J. (1963), *National Leadership and Foreign Policy: The Mobilization of Public Support*. Princeton, N.J.: Princeton University Press.

Rosenau, J. (1961), *Public Opinion and Foreign Policy*. New York: Random House.

Whitley, R. (1976), "Umbrellan and Polytheistic Scientific Disciplines and Their Elites," *Social Studies of Science 6*, 471.

Zuckerman, H. (1977), *Scientific Elite*. New York: Free Press.

Part 2

Empirical Studies

Barbara Desow Melber

5. Supply Versus Demand Energy Alternatives: Public Attitudes Toward Resource Conservation

Abstract

This chapter discusses general attitudes toward energy production and conservation alternatives, and their relationship to environmental, economic, and societal growth issues. The data presented are based on an analysis of approximately 50 national probability surveys conducted between 1972 and 1979. Findings from a small number of surveys conducted within the first three months following the nuclear power reactor accident at Three Mile Island are compared with trends prior to the accident. It is concluded that there is an indication of a trend toward greater public concern over the pace of economic growth and the related demands for resources and energy. Significant expansion of the energy industry is thus likely to continue to be under close public scrutiny and skepticism. However, the likelihood of the public participating in extensive conservation, which would limit the demand for greater energy production, is at this point quite questionable.

Introduction

This chapter focuses on trends in public attitudes toward energy. After a brief examination of general perceptions regarding growth and resource depletion, public preferences regarding alternative energy sources and energy production versus energy conservation strategies will be discussed. Change over time will be documented, with particular attention given to trends prior to and following the nuclear power reactor accident at Three Mile Island. Finally, relationships of environmental priorities and orientations toward growth to these broad energy perspectives will be examined.

The findings are based on an analysis of approximately fifty national probability surveys conducted between 1972 and 1979. The studies were conducted by many of the major national survey organizations of the United States as part of their regular assessments of public opinion on topics of social, economic, and political interest. These sources include Becker Research Corporation, Cambridge Reports, Inc., Gallup Poll, Louis Harris and Associates, Resources for the Future, Response Analysis Corporation, Roper Reports, Survey Research Laboratory, and Yankelovich, Skelly, and White, Inc. The data were obtained for a study of public attitudes toward nuclear power sponsored by the United States Department of Energy (Melber et al., 1979). A brief description of the sample, design, and content of the surveys cited in this article is provided in the appendix.

Orientations Toward Growth and Resource Consumption

Positions on the necessity of limiting growth and reducing the rate of resource consumption are quite split within the United States population. In 1978, close to 40 percent of respondents felt that resource depletion required a zero growth rate, while another 40 percent disagreed that such a limit was necessary. The remaining 20 percent were undecided. There has been a small degree of change in public response to this issue since 1975, with approximately a 10 percent increase in uncertainty and an 8 percent decrease in support for unlimited growth. In other measures of concern over high rates of growth and of resource usage, about 60 percent of the public agreed that resource consumption must be reduced or the country would "face disaster in a few years," and about 45 percent thought the growth rate should be decreased while approximately 40 percent disagreed. Aside from greater support for continued growth as income level increases, there are no important demographic differences on this issue. A consistent regional difference, however, is apparent, with residents of the Pacific states (California, Oregon, and Washington) least supportive of high rates of growth; for example, over 70 percent of these respondents agreed that resource consumption must be reduced and about 60 percent thought that a slow down in the growth rate would be beneficial. There has been a considerable decrease in the percentage of the population considering the recent shortages of energy and raw materials as only a temporary phenomenon, from 60 percent agreeing with this position in 1975 to approximately 40 percent agreeing in 1978 (Cambridge Reports, Inc.). Belief in the long-term nature of these problems appears to be gaining adherents within the general public.

One resource issue that has been recognized as having critical importance is that of energy. The general public has been personally affected by supply disruptions and dramatically rising prices in recent years. While the level of concern over supply shortages has fluctuated considerably over time, there is evidence of a gradual increase in belief in the seriousness of energy shortage problems. As shown in Figure 1, data from Louis Harris and Associates indicate a rapid decline in serious concern following the end of the oil embargo, from 50 percent of the public saying the situation was very serious in December of 1973 to between 22 percent to 34 percent throughout the following year. An average of about 45 percent of respondents perceived the situation as very serious in 1975 and 1976, and approximately 50 percent did so in 1977 and 1978, returning to the level of concern reported during the oil embargo of 1973.

The issues of greatest significance to the public in terms of the energy situation, however, appear to be those of increasing prices and dependence on foreign countries, rather than energy supply shortages per se. Data from Yankelovich, Skelly, and White (1978) indicate a high level of concern with both energy costs (the proportion of the public concerned increasing from 63 percent to 70 percent between 1976-1978) and foreign dependence (increasing from 53 percent to 63 percent). Concern over energy shortages, both within the next two years and within 20 to 25 years, has remained stable during this period, at about the 45 percent level. A further indication of the limited concern over immediate shortage problems is seen in data spanning 1974 through 1978 which indicate that a majority of the public believes that the shortage of electricity and gasoline has been exaggerated and is not serious; approximately 45 percent of the public also said that heating oil and natural gas shortages have been exaggerated (Yankelovich, Skelly, and White 1978).

Thus, while there is recognition of a serious energy situation in the United States, the problem of an absolute resource shortage is not perceived as the critical element. The cost and control of available supplies are the major concerns of the public. In the following sections, public assessments of alternative energy strategies will be documented, and the implications of these assessments for resource conservation will be examined.

Alternative Energy Source Preferences

The public has been most supportive of solar energy development. Over 80 percent of the public, a very high

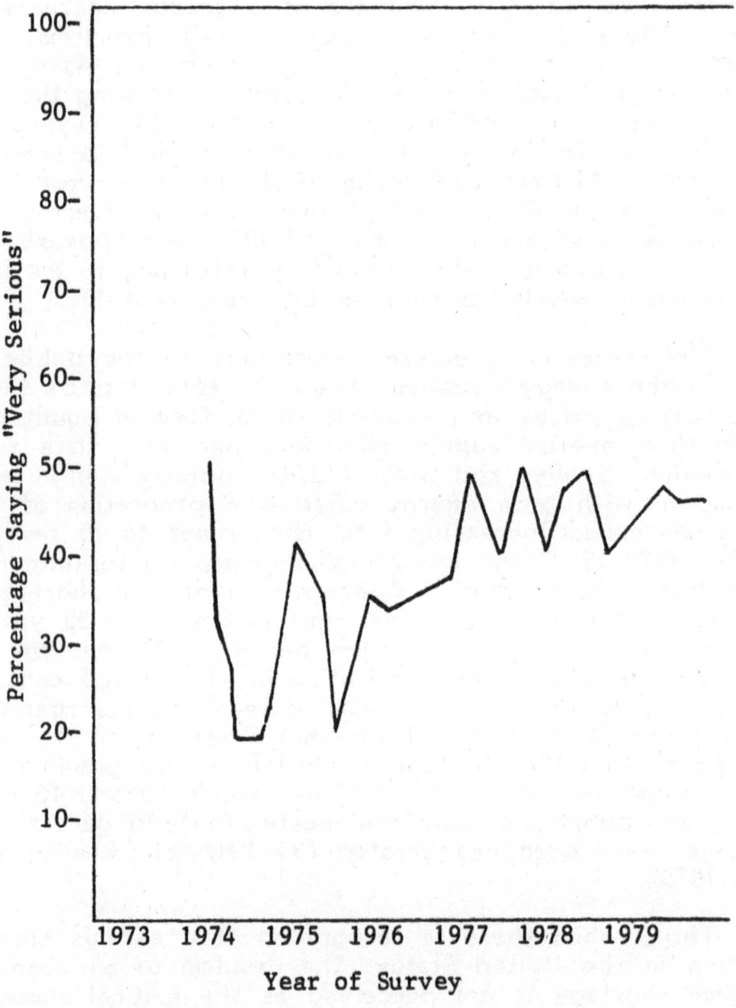

Figure 1. Seriousness of the Energy Shortage.

Source: Louis Harris and Associates: "How serious do you feel the energy shortage is in this country--very serious, only somewhat serious, or hardly serious at all?"

consensus, favored speeding up the development of solar energy in surveys conducted by Harris (76/7; 78/10). This compares to means of 69 percent supportive of offshore oil drilling, 60 percent favorable towards nuclear power plant construction, and 49 percent supportive of increased strip mining during that period (Harris 76/7; 78/10).

In most instances there was little change in public sentiment toward energy sources through 1978. Fluctuations have occurred, but without a clear direction. This was true of *general* levels of support for nuclear power which ranged from 44 percent to 63 percent throughout the 1970s, until the Three Mile Island accident (see Figure 2). Favorability toward *local* nuclear power plants, however, had been in decline during this period. Data from Response Analysis Corporation show a continuous decrease in support (from 55 percent in 1975 to 43 percent in 1978) and increase in opposition (from 32 percent in 1975 to 41 percent in 1978) toward community nuclear power plants. Both general and local acceptance of nuclear power declined sharply after the Three Mile Island accident, although the duration of this impact differs across survey organizations. While Harris surveys indicated a rebound in support as early as June, 1979, surveys conducted by Cambridge Reports continued to indicate very low levels of favorability at that time. Both Harris and Cambridge found relatively high levels of opposition to nuclear power (over 40 percent) through June, 1979 (see Figure 2).

Another significant trend concerning changes in the relative preferences of the public for energy sources is the increasing acceptance of coal. Coal had been one of the least desirable energy sources in the early 1970s. For example, Harris (75/4, 76/7;) found approximately 45 percent support for increasing strip mining between 1973 and 1976, and Cambridge (76/4; 76/7; 76/10; 76/12) found about 20 percent support for increased strip mining "even if it damages the environment," and about 25 percent support for converting electric utilities to coal "even if it means dirtier air" in 1976. There is some evidence of increased favorability toward coal since 1977. Cambridge (77/3; 77/6; 77/9; 77/11; 78/3; 78/8; 78/9; 78/11; 79/3) found a mean increase of approximately 10% support for both strip mining and coal conversion in studies conducted from 1977 through March 1979, relative to 1976 levels.

Figure 3 indicates the extent to which the public considered nuclear energy and coal as a "reliable form of energy for the U.S. to depend on in the long run" between 1975 and 1979 (Harris 75/6; 76/7; 78/10; 79/4). In 1975

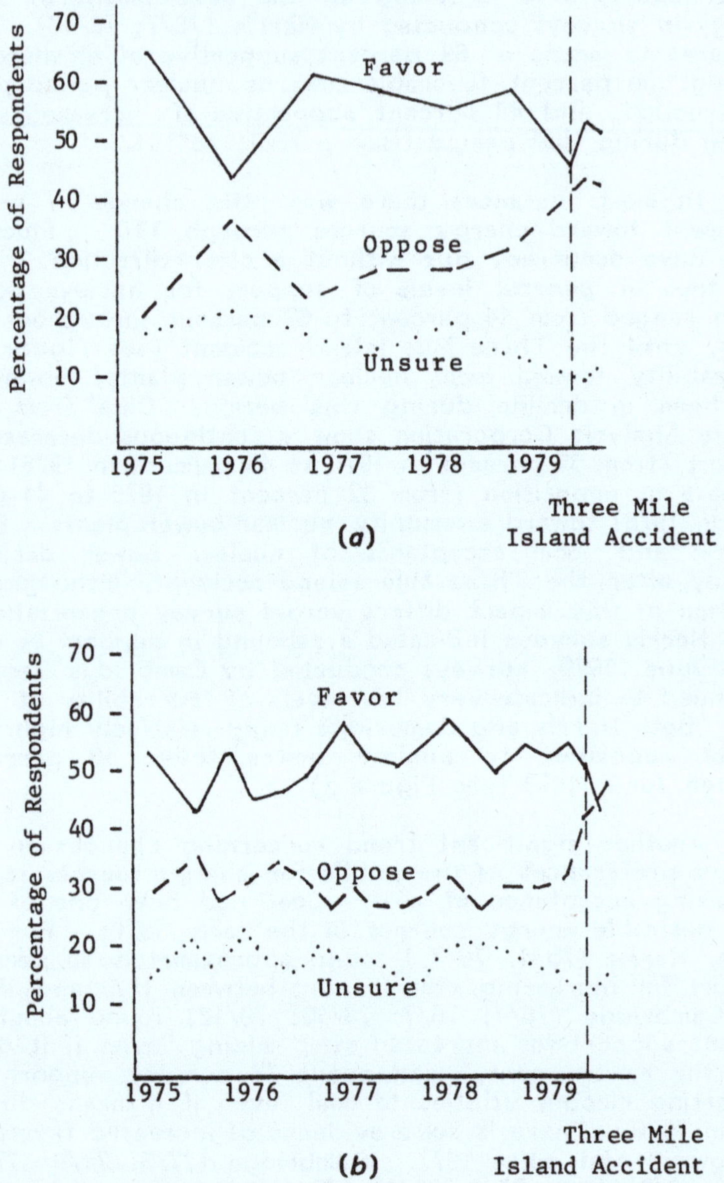

Figure 2. Construction of More Nuclear Power Plants: Trends Over Time.

Sources: (*a*) Louis Harris and Associates: "In general, do you favor or oppose the building of more nuclear power plants in the United States?". (*b*) Cambridge Reports, Inc.: "Do you favor or oppose the construction of more nuclear power plants?".

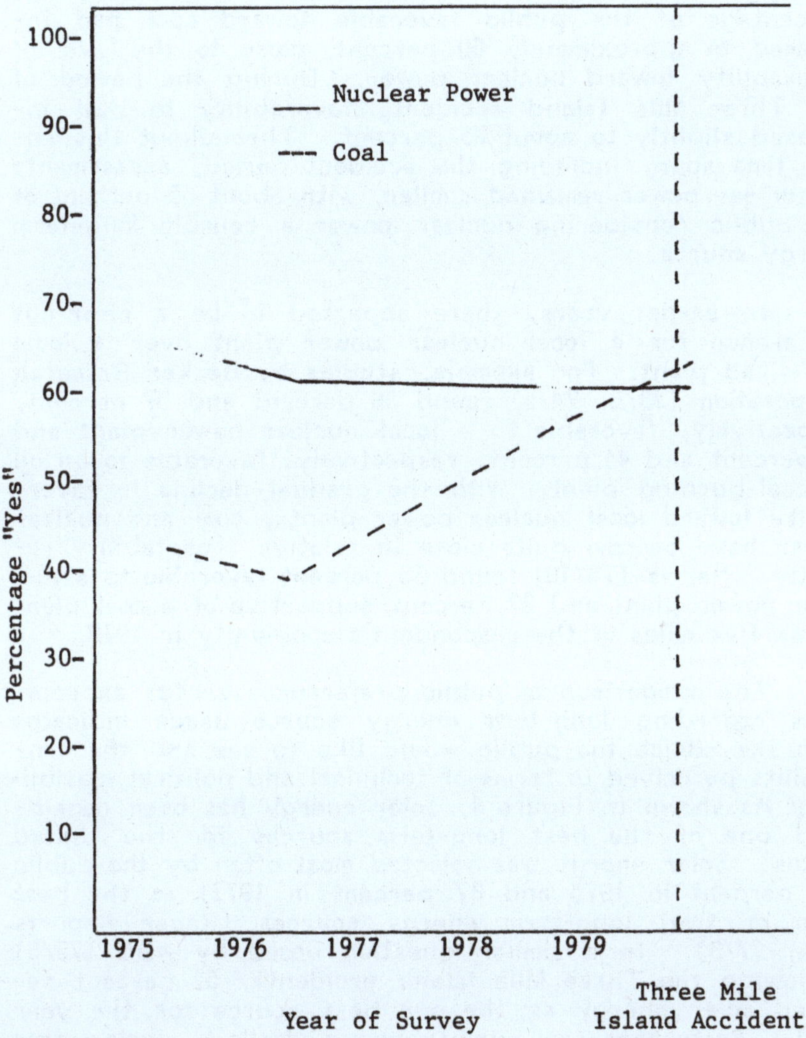

Figure 3. Coal and Nuclear Power as Long-Term Reliable Energy Sources.

Source: Louis Harris and Associates: "Do you think coal (nuclear power) is a reliable form of energy for the U.S. to depend upon in the long run?".

and 1976 about 45 percent of the public considered coal a reliable long-term source compared to about 65 percent considering nuclear power a reliable source. By 1978, the percentage of the public favorable toward coal had increased to approximately 60 percent, close to the level of favorability toward nuclear power. During the period of the Three Mile Island accident, favorability to coal increased slightly to about 65 percent. Throughout this entire time span, including the accident period, assessments of nuclear power remained similar, with about 65 percent of the public considering nuclear power a reliable long-term energy source.

In earlier years, there appeared to be a clear-cut preference for a local nuclear power plant over a local coal-fired plant. For example, studies by Becker Research Corporation (73/6; 74/5) found 56 percent and 57 percent, respectively, favorable to a local nuclear power plant and 37 percent and 44 percent, respectively, favorable to an oil or coal-burning plant. With the gradual decline in favorability toward local nuclear power plants, coal and nuclear power have become quite close in relative acceptability recently. Harris (78/10) found 35 percent favorable to a nuclear power plant and 37 percent supportive of a coal plant within five miles of the respondent's community in 1978.

The comparison of public preferences versus expectations regarding long-term energy source usage indicates both the choice the public would like to see and the constraints perceived in terms of technical and political feasibility. As shown in Figure 4, solar energy has been considered one of the best long-term sources for the United States. Solar energy was selected most often by the public (50 percent in 1975 and 67 percent in 1977) as the best (one or two) long-term energy sources (Roper Reports 75/4; 77/3). In a similar question posed by NBC (79/5) (following the Three Mile Island accident), 52 percent selected solar energy as the *one* best source for the year 2000. Preference for nuclear power declined during this period, from 47 percent in 1975 to 35 percent in 1977 selecting nuclear as one of the *two* best sources; only 16 percent of the public thought it would be the *one* best source for the future in May, 1979. It is interesting to note the low levels of preference for coal in the long-term, in spite of increased acceptance of coal use in recent years. Only about 20 percent of the public has considered coal one of the best long-term energy sources (see Figure 4).

Predictions regarding the actual dominance of various supply sources indicate a higher expected role for nuclear power and a lesser role for solar energy than the public would prefer, with over one-quarter expecting nuclear power and about one-third expecting solar energy to be the major electrical energy source in the year 2000 (see Figure 4). Less than 10 percent of the public expects coal to dominate the United States energy supply at that time (Cambridge Reports 77/11; Harris 78/10; 79/4).

Evaluations of the specific characteristics of a number of alternative energy sources indicate different types of advantages and disadvantages with each source. There is not any one source that is rated best on all characteristics. Evaluations of coal have been more positive in recent years, particularly in terms of supply assessments. Belief that there is an "almost unlimited" supply of coal increased from 44 percent in 1975 to 61 percent in 1979, and awareness of the domestic availability of coal and consequent reduced foreign dependence increased from 69 percent in 1975 to over 80 percent in 1978 (Harris 78/10; 79/4). These findings are consistent with the reported increase in public acceptance of coal over the past two years. Coal also is rated highly in terms of its cost. However, it continues to be evaluated as the least desirable source in terms of environmental consequences. Approximately 40 percent of the public considers coal the energy source most harmful to the environment, when compared to nuclear power, oil, hydroelectric power, and solar energy (Response Analysis Corporation 75/8; 77/8).

Nuclear power continues to be rated highly in terms of its supply characteristics; approximately three-fourths of the public think that nuclear energy is readily available in both the near and far term and is an energy source which reduces dependence on foreign suppliers. There was no evidence of a change in these supply assessments following the Three Mile Island accident (Harris 78/10; 79/4). Nuclear power is considered a more desirable energy source than coal or oil, but less desirable than solar energy or hydroelectric power in terms of environmental impacts (Response Analysis Corporation 75/8; 77/8). However, it is seen as more dangerous than both oil and coal in terms of health and safety risks (Harris 78/10; 79/4). Nuclear power also is believed to be one of the more expensive energy sources. While oil was rated the most expensive source by 30 percent of the public, 21 percent selected nuclear power and 20 percent chose natural gas as the most expensive source in a survey conducted by Response Analysis Corporation (77/8).

Solar energy is rated as the best source in terms of environmental effects, with close to 50 percent of the public

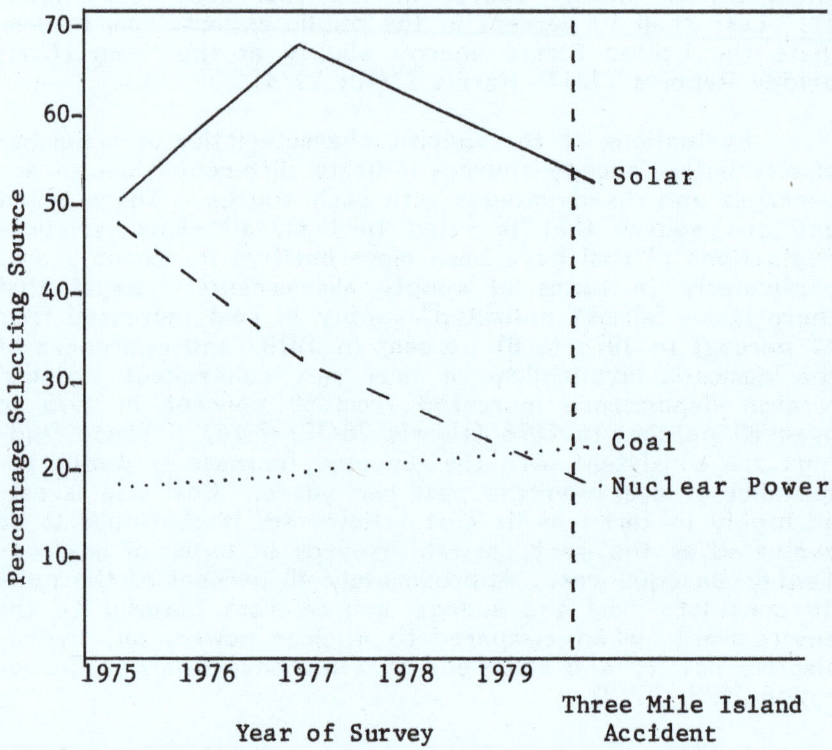

Figure 4. (*a*) Preferred Source(s) for the Year 2000.

Sources: Roper Reports (1975, 1977): "Looking ahead to the year 2000, which of these sources do you think offers the best long-term source of energy? Which one or two do you think we should spend the greatest effort on the development--coal, water power, ocean tids, wind power, solar energy?". NBC (1979): "Which one of these sources do you think is the best energy source for the United States in the year 2000--oil, coal, nuclear power, solar energy, hydroelectric power, natural gas?".

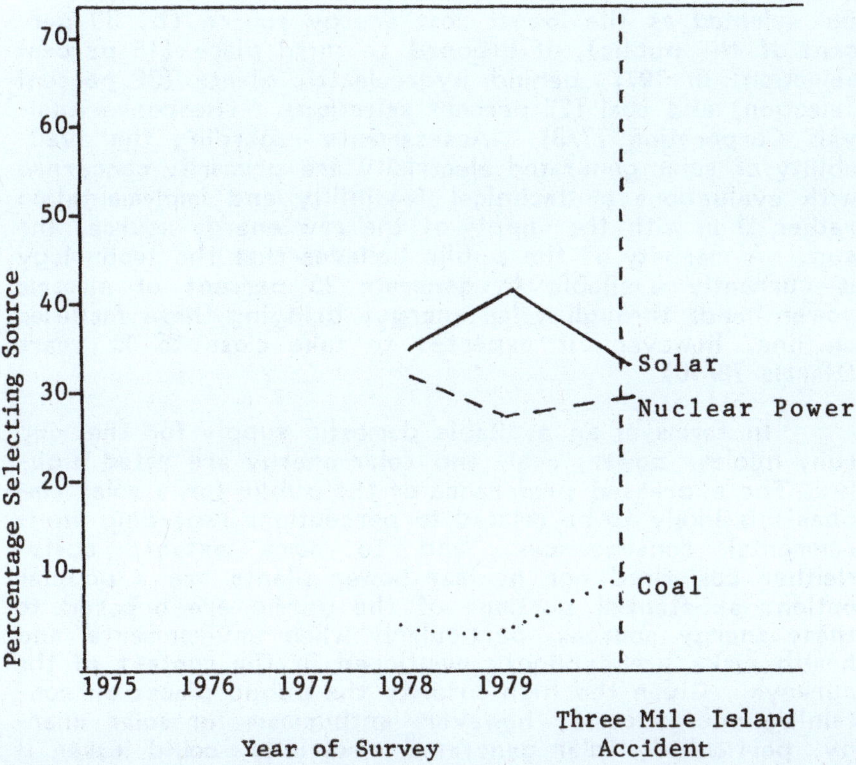

Figure 4. (*b*) Source Expected to Provide Most of Energy Supply for the Year 2000.

Sources: Cambridge Reports, Inc. (1977): "Which of the sources of power on this card--oil, coal, nuclear power, solar energy, hydroelectric power, natural gas--will be used most in 25 years?". Louis Harris and Associates (1978, 1979): "Which one of these fuels--oil, coal, nuclear power, solar energy, hydroelectic power, natural gas--do you think will supply most--say over 25 percent-of our electrical energy needs more than 20 years from now?".

selecting it as the least harmful energy source, compared to nuclear power, coal, oil, natural gas, and hydroelectric plants (Response Analysis Corporation 75/8; 77/8). Cost evaluations appear to have changed recently. While in a Cambridge Reports study (75/4) solar energy was most often selected as the lowest cost energy source (by 30 percent of the public), it dropped to third place (18 percent selection) in 1977, behind hydroelectric plants (36 percent selection) and coal (25 percent selection). (Response Analysis Corporation 77/8). Assessments regarding the availability of solar generated electricity are primarily concerned with evaluations of technical feasibility and implementation rather than with the supply of the raw energy source, the sun. A majority of the public believes that the technology is currently available to generate 25 percent of electric power needs through solar energy; bringing these facilities on line, however, is expected to take close to 15 years (Harris 78/10).

In terms of an available domestic supply for the long run, nuclear power, coal, and solar energy are rated highly. The expressed preference of the public for a solar emphasis is likely to be related to perceptions regarding environmental consequences, and to some extent, costs. Neither coal-fired nor nuclear power plants are a popular option; substantial portions of the public are opposed to these energy sources, particularly when environmental and health risks are explicitly mentioned in the context of the surveys. Given the high priority the public places on containing energy costs, however, enthusiasm for solar energy, particularly solar generated electricity, could lessen if the price of such energy is considerably higher than that of other sources.

Supply Versus Demand Energy Orientation

While public reactions to specific energy sources involve assessments of the characteristics of the particular source, they also may reflect the position of the public (or segments of the public) on a broader issue: a general energy perspective which emphasizes increasing the energy supply, or conversely, reducing energy demand. These approaches clearly are not mutually exclusive, but a tendency to focus on one strategy is likely, with certain segments of the public emphasizing production, while others stress the conservation alternative.

There is some evidence of an increase in concern with energy production recently. The percentage of the public preferring an "all out" effort to increase production to a similar effort to reduce energy usage rose from 41 percent in 1977 to 57 percent in 1978. Approximately one-third of the public favored the conservation approach in both years, suggesting that the change primarily was due to those who were unsure becoming more concerned about energy availability (Harris 78/10). The context of the emphasis on energy production, however, has changed markedly during the decade of the 1970s. Support for energy growth and unrestricted energy consumption was very high as late as 1973 -- only a few years ago. Since that time, there has been a shift to concern with limiting "unnecessary" energy usage. For example, the proportion of the public considering high levels of electricity growth (usage doubling in a ten year period) undesirable increased from only about 25 percent in 1971 to 1973 to over 60 percent in 1976 and 1977 (Response Analysis Corporation 77/8). In addition, as shown in Figure 5, the position of the public has reversed regarding building new power plants to allow unrestricted energy usage as opposed to reducing consumption to limit the need for new plants, from over 60 percent favoring such construction in 1973 to about 35 percent favorable between 1975 and 1978 (Response Analysis Corporation 78/8). Thus, current majority support for energy production is in terms of providing a sufficient supply, whereas formerly energy growth was supported without restriction. Public debate and controversy are thus likely to center on determining what levels of energy consumption are "necessary" and desirable for American society.

In recent years, a conservation emphasis has been seen as important by an increasing percentage of the United States population. However, this attitude trend has not been associated with significant shifts in the behavior patterns of most Americans in terms of energy consumption habits. In 1977, almost two-thirds of the public said that energy conservation was very important; there were few demographic differences on this issue, except by gender, with women more likely than men to see a strong need for energy conservation (Response Analysis Corporation 77/8). In response to a list of reasons for current energy problems, 63 percent of the public considered wasteful use of energy by most Americans as a major cause compared to approximately 50 percent selecting OPEC oil prices, delay in alternative energy source production, and lack of a federal energy policy, as very important factors (Harris 78/10). Only one-third however, felt that household conservation could have a major impact on national levels of energy consumption (Cambridge 78/8).

Trend data on reported conservation behavior indicate very little change between 1974 through 1978. Most indi-

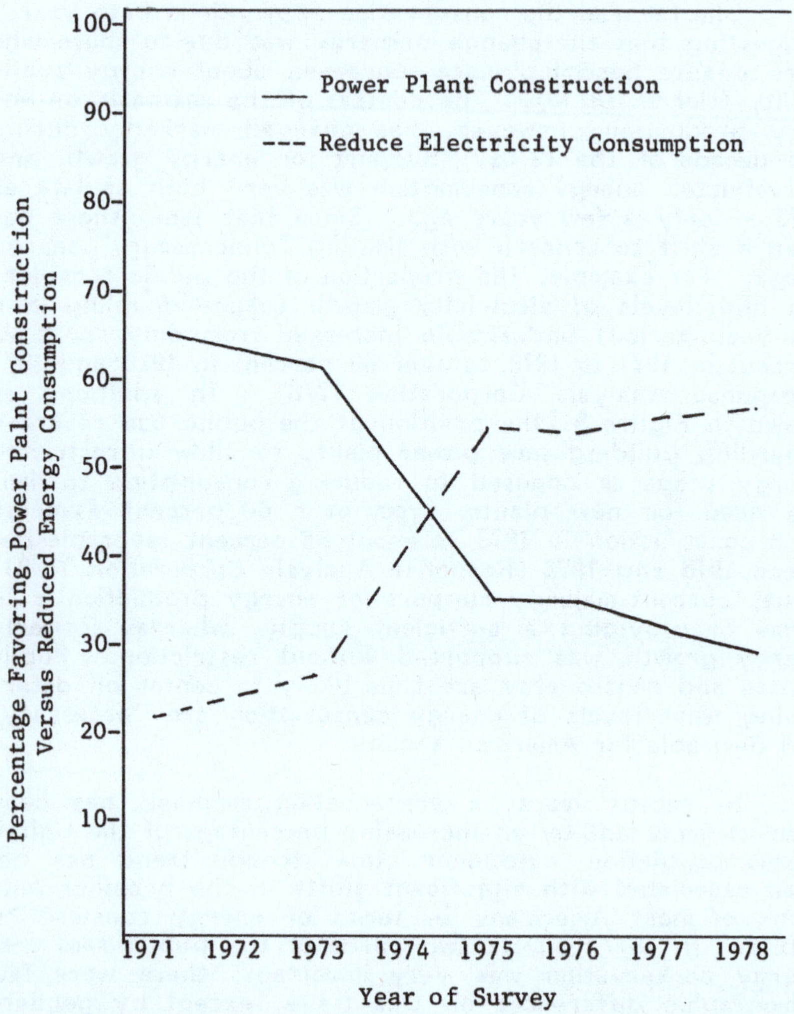

Figure 5. Power Plant Construction Versus Reducing Electricity Consumption.

Source: Response Analysis Corporation: "Which of these two things do you think is better: to build as many new power plants as are needed to let everyone use all the electricity they want, or to try to limit or cut back the use of electricity so that fewer new plants will have to be built?".

viduals (over 70 percent) say they are attempting to reduce energy usage, but there are very few actions reported by a majority of the public. Lower heat thermostat settings and slower driving speeds are the most commonly reported conservation behaviors (by 73 percent and 60 percent of the public, respectively). Approximately 30 percent report purchasing a smaller car or installing insulation; only 15 percent indicate greater use of mass transit or car pools (Yankelovich, Skelly, and White, 1978).

There is considerable support for government intervention to encourage conservation when the costs are of an indirect rather than direct nature. For example, two-thirds of the public supports expansion of mass transit via increased taxes and the use of energy tax revenues (Cambridge Reports 77/3). A majority also supports tax rebates for conservation activities such as installing insulation or storm windows, although a majority is opposed to a tax on low mileage automobile purchases (Gallup 77/3).

There is also strong opposition to use of higher prices as a mechanism to increase energy conservation. Regulations and rationing are preferred to across-the-board price increases. Findings from Gallup and Cambridge surveys indicate 60 percent to 70 percent opposition to increased energy prices. In a specific trade-off question, 65 percent of respondents preferred gasoline rationing (to three-quarters of current usage) compared to 15 percent who preferred a gasoline price increase to $2.00 per gallon (Cambridge).

There is a substantial gap between support for the idea of conservation, such as government investment in mass transit, and actual reported energy conservation behavior. While most of the public reports some type of conservation activity, it is generally of a very limited nature. Thus, while there is public support for government efforts to increase voluntary conservation, there is not much evidence that this would be an effective approach to reducing energy demand.

Conservation is likely to be an attractive alternative to the public because it is seen as allowing domestic control and price containment. In a 1977 Cambridge Reports survey, close to 60 percent of the public thought that energy conservation would be a "cheaper solution for the U.S. in the long run" than energy development. While about 45 percent of the public agreed that depending on conservation to solve the energy crisis would result in a lower standard of living, 60 percent did not expect their own personal

Table 1. Support for air pollution control

Respondent Category	Level of Support* (%)		
	Strong	Moderate	Weak
Total	45	44	11
Sex			
Men	40	47	13
Women	50	40	10
Age			
Under 30	52	38	10
39-49	44	45	11
50 and over	40	48	12
Region			
Northeast	51	41	8
North Central	40	48	12
South	42	46	12
West	52	35	13

*Level of support for controlling air pollution, 1978 (Yankelovich, Skelly, and White)

standard of living to be affected by such a conservation program (Cambridge). Given the strong and consistent opposition to a pricing approach to conservation, the public is likely to be much more responsive to a mandatory rationing program that is seen as spreading the burden of change more equitably across the entire population than would be achieved by a market mechanism.

The Influence of Environmental Priorities on Energy Orientations

Concern over environmental pollution continues to be widespread among the American public. Surveys conducted by Harris and Yankelovich, Skelly, and White during the 1970s indicate that over 60 percent of the public considers air and water pollution very serious problems. Trend data for 1974 to 1978 from Yankelovich indicate no change in public support for pollution control efforts; 45 percent to 50 percent of the public strongly supported such efforts, 40 percent to 45 percent indicated moderate support, and 10 percent showed weak levels of support. Demographic breakdowns, shown in Table 1, indicate that women tend to be more concerned with environmental protection than men, younger (under age 30) respondents show greater concern than older respondents, and residents of the Northeast and the West are more concerned than residents of the other regions of the country.

While strong support for efforts to improve environmental quality has been maintained, conflicts between energy consumption and production and environmental protection have become increasingly apparent in recent years. The conflicts involve both energy supply and energy price issues. In terms of supply, there are two concerns. First, energy production is often associated with increased environmental pollution; for example, the burning of coal increases air pollution. Second, environmental protection often requires the use of greater amounts of energy, as in the case of pollution control devices for automobiles which result in higher rates of gasoline consumption. The price conflict is due to the cost of environmental protection strategies to minimize pollution from energy production which lead to increased energy prices, creating a trade-off between higher energy costs and environmental quality.

A number of survey organizations have posed questions involving trade-offs between environmental quality and energy availability. Roper Reports has tracked public response to a choice between assuring adequate energy supplies versus protecting the environment. As indicated in

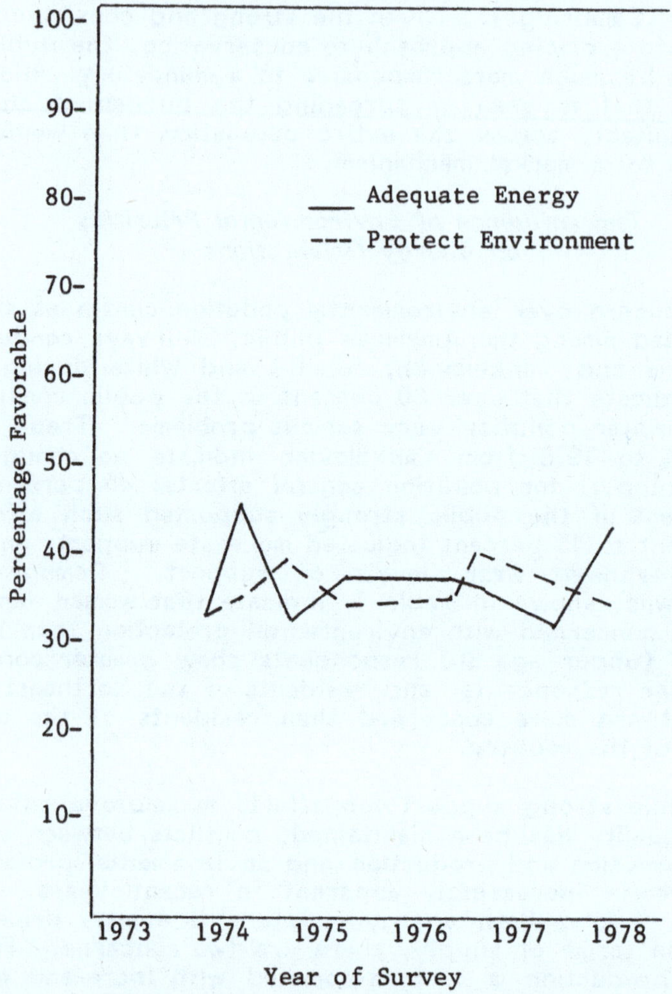

Figure 6. Energy Versus Environment.

Source: Roper Reports: "There is continuing talk about an energy crisis and the idea that there won't be enough electricity and other forms of energy to meet consumer demands in the coming years. Some people say that the progress of this nation depends on an adequate supply of energy and we have to have it even if it means taking some risks with the environment. Others say the important thing is the environment, and that it is better to risk not having enough energy than to risk spoiling our environment. Are you more on the side of adequate energy or more on the side of protecting the environment?'

Figure 6, the public has been split over which of these deserves higher priority. Emphasis on energy has been greatest during the 1973 oil embargo and the severe winter of 1977.

There is some evidence of a recent increase in public willingness to relax environmental protection efforts if this would result in increased energy availability. Harris reported only 25 percent support for (and 65 percent to 70 percent opposition to) this approach in 1975 and 1976, but 45 percent support (and 42 percent opposition) in 1978. Both Response Analysis Corporation and Resources for the Future, however, found greater support for environmental protection (51 percent and 47 percent, respectively) than for energy supply (40 percent and 31 percent, respectively) in similar trade-off questions posed in 1978. Gallup and Harris data from the spring and summer of 1979 indicate majority support for relaxing specific environmental protection regulations (such as allowing use of leaded gasoline) in order to increase energy availability.

There appears to be little support for paying higher energy prices to reduce pollution. In 1978 less than 25 percent of the public favored electricity price increases for reclaiming strip mined land or air pollution control devices for coal burning power plants (Yankelovich, Skelly, and White). A study of several communities across the United States by the Survey Research Laboratory found that respondents who were younger (under age 30) or who had high income or educational levels were most willing to pay increased energy costs (an additional 10 percent to 25 percent) for environmental protection. Residents from the West (Washington and Wyoming) were also more supportive of price increases for such protection than those from the Midwest (Michigan and Illinois).

These various and at times conflicting findings indicate the difficulty of choosing between the desire for a high level of environmental quality and the concern with sufficient energy supplies. There does appear to be a recent shift toward energy production, with a greater willingness than in earlier years to relax some environmental controls. However, there is still a wide split within the public on this issue, and it is not clear whether these recent results are merely another short-term fluctuation or the beginning of a more stable trend.

An examination of the relationship of environmental priorities to resource and energy issues, based on secondary analysis of a 1978 survey conducted by Cambridge Re-

Table 2. Economic growth versus environmental quality

Belief in Trade-off*	Forced Choice Preference (%)**		
	Sacrifice Environment	Unsure	Sacrifice Economic Growth
Total (100%)	23	39	37
Can have both economic growth and environmental quality (47%)	30	37	33
Unsure (23%)	11	77	12
Must sacrifice one (30%)	22	17	60

*Source: Cambridge Reports: "Which of these two statements is closest to your opinion: there is no relationship between economic growth and the quality of the environment -- indeed, we can have more and more goods and services and also a clean world; or we cannot have both economic growth and a high level of environmental quality, we must sacrifice one or the other."

**Source: Cambridge Reports: "Which of these two statements is closer to your opinion: we must be prepared to sacrifice environmental quality for economic growth; we must sacrifice economic growth in order to preserve and protect the environment."

ports (78/6), indicates that individuals who are most concerned with environmental problems tend to favor a slow down in general growth due to resource depletion and show greater opposition than individuals with lower levels of environmental concern, to an energy production emphasis (including strip mining coal, coal conversion of utilities, nuclear power plant construction, and hydroelectric power dam construction). While the correlations between these attitudes are significant ($p < .05$), they are generally small in magnitude, around the .2 level. There was no relationship between level of environmental concern and reported conservation behavior.

Conflict between environmental protection and economic growth has also been an issue, since industrial growth is often associated with pollution. Data from Cambridge Reports indicate that close to half of the public does not think that economic growth necessarily conflicts with environmental quality while 30 percent think a trade-off is necessary (see Table 2). When asked to choose between environmental quality and economic growth, 37 percent selected environmental quality, 23 percent chose economic growth, 39 percent were unsure. The very large percentage of undecided respondents is unusual; typically "don't know" responses are only at the 15 percent to 20 percent level. Even among the highly educated and high income groups (those most likely to take a position on issues), about one-third were unsure. These findings suggest that the trade-off is a very difficult one, and that there is considerable ambivalence on this issue. Those who feel the United States can have both environmental quality and economic growth are evenly split when forced to choose between the two, while there is a clear preference for environmental protection at the expense of economic growth among those who feel a trade-off is necessary (see Table 2). There appears to be little support for sacrificing environmental quality. The highest preference of any respondent group willing to make the environmental sacrifice was 29 percent among residents of the industrial North and South. Respondents under 35 years of age were the most willing to forego economic growth; about 45 percent of this group would sacrifice economic growth for environmental protection. Whether or not this age relationship reflects a cohort as well as an age effect cannot be determined at this time. A pure age effect indicates that younger people are more willing to sacrifice economic growth, but as they age they would incline more favorably toward economic growth. A cohort effect implies that the experience of the younger group in the last decade of increased environmental awareness will continue to influence their positions as they age, so they will be less likely to take on the attitudes that older groups currently express. The cohort effect thus would suggest that over time an increasing percentage of the population would become more environmentally concerned.

Conclusion

What are the implications of these public orientations for resource conservation in the area of energy? The most significant change in public attitudes has been a reversal of the pre 1973 assumption that growth in energy consumption was a good in itself. There is now majority support for curtailment of energy usage, and a dominant view that Americans are wasteful in their energy consumption patterns. It is also apparent that there is considerable disenchantment with many of the currently available energy production alternatives, particularly nuclear power and coal. Support for environmental protection remains strong, although in acute energy supply situations, there is willingness to relax some controls on a short-term basis. Finally, increased energy prices are the greatest concern of the public, suggesting that any strategy involving very high direct costs to the public will be met with considerable opposition. Significant expansion of the energy industry is thus likely to continue to be under close public scrutiny and skepticism.

The conservation alternative appears to be consistent with public priorities since it may control costs without negative environmental consequences. Empirical evidence regarding actual conservation behavior, however, indicates that public participation in extensive voluntary conservation, which would limit the demand for energy expansion is unlikely. It is more likely that pressures for mandatory conservation regulations will continue to develop due to a combination of international events which disrupt the flow of energy supplies and domestic delay of power plant construction because of environmental and cost concerns. The majority of the public clearly prefers such controls to the alternative of higher prices to reduce energy demand.

Solar energy is the one production alternative that is perceived by the public as having the potential for significant energy expansion, without undesirable environmental consequences. The cost level of a solar energy emphasis is likely to be the major factor that would affect continued public enthusiasm for solar technology.

While the data on public attitudes provided in this paper indicate public preferences and concerns over a wide range of energy and environment issues, the ways in which this type of information can be useful for policy making also need to be directly addressed. Policy clearly is not made on the basis of majority public opinion; however, there are some specific uses of such information that can aid in policy decisions. First, since policy decisions usually involve some assumptions about what beliefs are held by the public and what public response might be, some foreknowledge of the range and variation in public attitudes and beliefs could be helpful in shaping specific programs. For example, the relatively low level of concern for energy shortages in terms of basic supply problem, and high level of concern over cost and foreign dependence, suggests that energy conservation and production programs based on limiting price increases and U.S. energy independence would be more successful than a general resource conservation approach. Second, active interest groups which attempt to influence government policy commonly view and present themselves as speaking for the general public will. Data on national trends in public attitudes can help place the positions of various interest groups in the context of the particular segments of the public that their view does in fact represent. Those who say there is a consensus for solar development are presenting an accurate picture, while those who claim the general public supports nuclear power expansion and only a small minority are opposed, are not making a valid statement. Third, public attitude data provide a measure of latent support and opposition to policies and programs. While most individuals queried in surveys will not take specific political action, information on the climate of opinion is useful for anticipating potential problems with implementation. A fourth type of use of public attitude and belief data is to identify areas for public education and information. For example, public expectations of solar energy, particularly in terms of cost, are very unrealistic given current estimates of solar technology.

The actual use of these types of data in the policy process is problematic for several reasons. Most basic is the problem of variation in findings, which allows selective use of survey data by interest groups to support a given position. While careful analysis of trends across survey organizations is likely to identify some consistent findings, the common practice of partial use of data for specific purposes leads to mistrust of the entire process. Thus, while public attitude data can be an important source of information for policy development, the misuse of this tool has led to a loss of credibility in its role of providing empirically sound data. A different problem is determining what the appropriate role of public attitude data is in setting policy. Public preference alone is not a justification for a specific action, although opposition may be sufficient for abandoning a given policy. Thus, it appears that the linkage of public attitude data to the policy process is in terms of the potential for opposition and problems of implementation, rather than a positive force in policy formation. The impact of general public opinion appears greatest through a veto role for specific policy decisions.

Reference

Melber, B. D., S. M. Nealey, C. S. Weiss, W. L. Rankin (1979), *Nuclear Power and the Public: Update of Collected Survey Research*. (Draft Report prepared for the U.S. Department of Energy) B-HARC-411-020. Batelle Human Affairs Research Center, Seattle.

Annotated Survey References

Becker (73/6) (74/5)

Becker Research Corporation, Boston, Massachusetts.

Sample and Design: National probability sample; 1,250-1,430 respondents; personal interviews.

General Content: Electric company services; general nuclear attitudes.

Nuclear Specific Content: General nuclear attitudes; nuclear plants nearby.

Demographic Information: Sex, age, education, income; geographic region, rural/urban.

Cambridge (75/5) (75/8) (75/12) (76/4) (76/7) (76/10) (76/12) (77/3) (77/5) (77/6) (77/9) (77/11) (78/3) (78/5) (78/6) (78/8) (78/9) (78/11) (79/3) (79/4) (79/6)

Cambridge Reports, Inc., Cambridge, Massachusetts.

Sample and Design: National probability sample; 1,500-2,000 respondents; personal interviews (79/4 survey, 800 respondents, telephone interviews).

General Content: Political issues; general energy issues -- conservation, economic growth, pollution, energy needs and shortages; alternative energy sources -- oil, coal, solar; general nuclear attitudes (varies across surveys).

Nuclear Specific Content: Waste disposal and storage, safety, cost, licensing, breeder reactor.

Demographic Information: Sex, age, education, income; geographic region, rural/urban.

Gallup (76/6) (79/4)

Gallup Poll, The Gallup Opinion Index, Princeton, New *Jersey*.

Sample and Design: National probability sample; 1,500 respondents; personal interviews.

General Content: General nuclear (76/6) (79/4); political issues (79/4).

Nuclear Specific Content: Attitudes toward nuclear power to meet energy needs; nuclear plants nearby; safety; knowledge; issues specific to the Three Mile Island incident (79/4).

Demographic Information: Sex, age, education, income, occupation; geographic region.

Gallup (77/2) (77/3)

The Gallup Organization, Inc., Princeton, New Jersey.

Sample and Design: National random sample; 1,000 respondents; telephone interviews.

General Content: Personal conservation behavior; impact of fuel shortages; concern about energy shortages; comparative technologies; general nuclear.

Nuclear Specific Content: Attitudes toward nuclear power plants in context of safety standards (77/3).

Demographic Information: Not available.

Gallup (79/7)

The Gallup Organization, Inc., Princeton, New Jersey.

Sample and Design: National random sample; 500 respondents; telephone interviews.

General Content: Energy vs. environmental tradeoffs.

Nuclear Specific Content: General attitude.

Demographic Information: Not available.

Harris (75/4) (76/7) (78/10)

Louis Harris and Associates, New York.

Sample and Design: National probability sample; 1,500 respondents; separate sample of leadership groups -- 325 respondents; personal interviews).

General Content: General energy concerns -- future energy needs, shortages, production versus conservation; alternative energy sources -- solar, oil, coal; environmental issues; credibility of information sources, general nuclear attitudes.

Nuclear Specific Content: Attitudes toward building nuclear power plants in the United States, to generate electricity, and within five miles of one's community; specific issues of waste storage and disposal, health, sabotage, accidents, inspection.

Demographic Information: Sex, race, age, education, income, occupation; geographic region, rural/urban.

Harris (79/4)

ABC News -- Harris Survey, New York, April 6-15, 1979.

Sample and Design: National probability sample; 1,500 respondents; personal interviews.

General Content: General energy issues -- oil shortages/dependence; general nuclear attitudes; nuclear specific issues.

Nuclear Specific Content: Attitudes toward nuclear plant construction; environmental danger -- water pollution, radiation danger, comparative danger with coal, oil; safety; Three Mile Island specific.

Demographic Information: Sex, race, age, education, income, occupation; geographic region, rural/urban.

RAC (75/8) (77/8) (78/8)

Response Analysis Corporation, Princeton, New Jersey.

Sample and Design: National probability sample; 1,000 respondents; personal interviews.

General Content: General energy issues -- atittudes toward the energy crisis, growth, environmental concerns, conservation; attitudes toward utility company rates and services; comparative technologies; general nuclear attitudes.

Nuclear Specific Content: Attitudes toward nuclear plant construction in local area; waste disposal, safety, pollution, radiation, accident, knowledge, long-term effects.

Demographic Information: Sex, age; geographic region, rural/urban.

RFF (78/8)

Resources for the Future (R.C. Mitchell), Washington, D.C.

Sample and Design: National random sample; 1,076 respondents; telephone interviews.

General Content: General social issues; general energy issues -- attitudes toward environmental groups and issues; general nuclear issues.

Nuclear Specific Content: Attitudes assessing general feelings toward nuclear power; trust in information sources.

Demographic Information: Not available.

Roper (73/10) (74/1) (74/5) (74/10) (75/4) (75/6) (75/8) (75/10) (76/1) (76/6) (76/8) (76/10) (76/11) (77/3) (77/9)

Roper Organization, Inc., New York. (Selected items made available by the Atomic Industrial Forum, Inc., Washington, D.C. and Solar Energy Research Institute, Golden, Colorado).

Sample and Design: National probability sample; 2,000 respondents; personal interviews.

General Content: General energy issues -- alternative energy sources; environmental issues, conservation; general nuclear issues; general political issues, general economic issues (varies across surveys).

Nuclear Specific Content: Attitudes toward nuclear power to meet energy needs; safety proliferation.

Demographic Information: Sex, age, education, income, occupation; geographic region, rural/urban.

SRL (76/6)

Survey Research Laboratory, University of Illinois.

Sample and Design: National probability sample; 1,400 respondents; personal interviews.

General Content: General energy issues; alternate energy sources -- primary focus on wind energy, also solar, coal, oil, and gas.

Nuclear Specific Content: Comparative preferences for nuclear and other energy sources.

Demographic Information: Sex, age, education, occupation, income.

YS&W (77) (78)

Yankelovich, Skelly, and White, Inc., New York.

Sample and Design: National probability sample; 2,000 respondents; samples of leadership groups; personal interviews.

General Content: General energy issues, economic, political, environmental issues.

Nuclear Specific Content: Attitudes toward nuclear plant construction; waste disposal, contamination, leakage, explosion, sabotage, theft.

Harry J. Otway

6. Risk Research and Its Relevance to Energy Planning

Abstract[1]

The treatment of risk has become an important issue in energy planning. It no longer seems possible or desirable to leave the issue in the hands of technical experts; attention must be paid to the values and beliefs of various public groups, thereby adding new complexities to the planning process. Researchers in the emerging field known as risk assessment have produced quantitative studies of technical risks and the social reactions to them. This chapter reviews the kinds of analyses that have been done, giving special emphasis to two empirical studies that demonstrate the measurement of "risk perceptions." The relevance of risk research results to regulatory policy making is discussed.

Introduction

Risk has become one of the central issues in the planning of energy strategies: the combustion of fossil fuels leads to the atmospheric CO_2 problem; oil recovery and transport can be accompanied by environmentally damaging spills while dependence upon imported oil is not without political risks; and the accident at Three Mile Island has served as a reminder of nuclear energy risks. Standards, the most common regulatory tool, were typically developed as part of a consensus-forming process between two actors--usually governmental and industry experts. They tended to be rather arbitrary at first, later assuming a more "scientific" character through an iterative process with increasing experience of the new technology (Holden, 1966; Majone, 1975). However, the complexity and magnitude of many new risks has posed new limits to the traditional learn-by-experience approach to the definition of their acceptability; in many cases calculation and judgment must now substitute for experience in what Weinberg has called "trans-science" (Weinberg, 1972).

Just as scientists became increasingly concerned about risk problems, various actors from the public sector also developed an awareness of their stakes in technical decisions and inserted themselves into the regulatory process, thereby upsetting the balance of this comfortable and functioning two-way power relationship. These public groups have brought their own (not always clearly articulated) values and beliefs into the process--values and beliefs which often differ from those of technocrats from either the industrial or government side. Thus it seems no longer possible, or desirable, to restrict discussions of risk to exclusively technical considerations of cost-benefit analysis or risk estimates. Instead, the acceptability of technological risks has become a confusing matter of political argumentation, power politics and negotiation.

The change from two-actor to three-actor model of regulation has added a new dimension to the uncertainties facing planners; many policies, based upon sound technical analyses, have nevertheless encountered severe and limiting opposition from the public. One response from the technical community was the appearance of quantitative studies of technical risks and of the social reactions to them. This chapter will trace the emergence of risk research as a new "discipline" by briefly reviewing the types of analyses which have been done under this heading; special emphasis will be given to a summary of two empirical studies which demonstrate the measurement of "risk perceptions." Finally, the relevance of risk research results to regulatory policy making will be discussed.

Risk Assessment

In general, risk researchers (Kates, 1976; Rowe; 1977, Otway and Pahner, 1976) have divided the area into three sub-topics: *risk estimation,* the identification and quantification of risks; *risk evaluation,* the measurement of public preference with respect to risk-taking; and *risk management,* organizational and procedural aspects of the integration of technical and social systems.

In practice, risk assessment has mostly involved the adoption and application of existing analytical methods, but because of its concern with social and management systems as well as technical matters, these methods have been applied in novel combinations. The analysts who carried out early technical risk studies tended to have a "hard science" orientation and came from professional fraternities which are, to a considerable extent, themselves defined by the confluence of interests of the particular regulator-industry actors involved.

Risk Estimation and Risk Perception

Most early risk estimation studies on energy systems (Starr, 1964; Farmer, 1967) concentrated on making quantitative estimates of mortality risk to members of the public, either from routine operations of a facility or from accidents. These estimates were usually put "in perspective" by comparing their magnitudes with statistical data on other, more familiar risks of daily life. Later, more extensive studies offered comparisons with both man-made and natural hazards as a function of frequency and magnitude of consequence (NRC, 1975), or comparisons amongst various types of energy systems (Inhaber, 1978). Studies of this type all had a strong technical flavour and were oriented toward aiding regulatory decision-making. The implication was that if the risks of a new activity were less than those of other, already accepted activities, then the new activity should also be acceptable; or, given the same benefits, the energy alternative with the lowest risk should be the rational choice.

But, in the event, new risks (i.e. the facilities or technologies which produce them) that *should* have been acceptable by this reasoning were not always accepted. As a result the term "risk perception" was coined by technologists to explain the observation that public reactions to new technologies often seemed to be "out of proportion" to the estimated levels of risk--people must be perceiving something about the risks, not captured in the quantitative expressions, that was causing them to behave risk aversively. The model of human behaviour implied by the risk perception concept went something like this: behaviours which reflect opposition to a technology *are* determined by (perhaps inaccurate) perceptions of its risks, but "risk perception" *should* be determined by "objective" risk data, its comparison with statistics on other risks, the "objective" benefits provided, and perhaps some additional qualitative information--such as whether risk exposure is voluntary or not (Starr, 1969). These assumed determinants of "risk perception" are largely of a quantitative technical nature (consistent with the technologists' way of thinking about technical matters) and were usually thought of as being fixed, i.e. the same--for every risk situation and for every social group.

But the technologists' intuitive behavioural model did not have predictive validity as evidenced by the continuing existence of "acceptance crises." Thus interest grew in risk evaluation: studies intended to identify the underlying determinants of "risk perception."

Risk Evaluation: Public Preferences

There are only two conceptually different approaches to obtain measures of public preferences with respect to technological risks (Fischhoff, 1978b): either retrospective examination of the manifest choices made by society in similar situations in the past, called revealed preferences, or the elicitation of currently expressed preferences, obtained directly through interviews or surveys. Although the revealed preferences method has the advantage of dealing with actual behaviours which have taken place in real situations, there are severe limitations imposed by the basic premises of the method (Lagadac, 1977; Fischhoff, 1978a; Otway, et al, 1975). These limitations will not be discussed in depth here, however; for our purposes it is enough to note that the method is not sensitive enough to provide differential information on the determinants of risk perception, and it is these underlying reasons for differing perceptions that are of most interest. A review of social science methods related to the elicitation of preferences suggests that risk perception can be well expressed as an *attitude,* thus allowing it to be understood and interpreted in the light of the theoretical constructs and methods provided by more than 40 years of attitude research.

The Attitude Concept

Attitude may be defined as an evaluative judgment of the degree to which one likes or dislikes some person, object, concept or symbol, i.e. a *feeling* of favourableness or unfavourableness toward the "object" of the attitude. Since the term risk perception emerged to describe people's *feelings* about risks, it satisfies the definition of attitude if the risk in question is considered to be the attitude object.

Attitudes are built upon the *beliefs* which are held about the attitude object. Beliefs are simply the "learned" relationships between the attitude object and its perceived attributes, or characteristics, e.g. John (the attitude object) is generous (an attribute). The strength of belief, which may be thought of as a subjective probability judgment, is related to the intensity of the learning experience. When the risk perception-attitude analogy is pursued then the beliefs which underlie attitude assume a special importance because they become the determinants of risk perception.

As we develop as individuals we learn through direct experience of the relationships amongst the objects and concepts which form our environment and thereby gradually build a view of the world. This picture will tend to be rather accurate, to the extent that the perceptual inputs are clear and based upon experience, but it follows that the experiences people will have will be different, in part due to restrictions imposed by the social and physical environments in which they find themselves. Since one rarely questions the validity of his own senses, *descriptive beliefs,* based upon personal experience with the attitude object, will be held with maximum certainty. We also receive *information* from other people which, to the extent it is accepted, enters into the formation of our system of beliefs. These beliefs are further extended by *inferential* processes based upon other beliefs already acquired. A belief system is thus formed which enables us to go beyond the information provided in a given situation to make predictions (inferences) about events and relationships which cannot be perceived and have never been experienced.

Figure 1, adapted from Fishbein and Ajzen (Fishbein and Ajzen, 1975), shows empirically supported (see Ajzen and Fishbein, 1977) relationships amongst beliefs, attitude and behaviours. A relatively large number of beliefs (usually thought to be in the range of 7 ± 2) are seen to underlie any given attitude, but this attitude is seen only to predispose a person to behave in a consistent way when the *totality* of his behaviours with respect to the attitude object are considered, i.e. attitude should not be expected to be a predictor of any one *specific* behaviour; all behaviours, taken together, will be consistent with the attitude. Now it becomes clear that the determinants of risk perception will be larger in number than technologists had originally expected, will vary from person to person, from one social group to the next and could be expected to include any perceived characteristics of a technology--non-technical as well as technical--if the former have played a significant role in the learning experience. Because this is a central issue in any discussion of the use of risk assessment results, the possible importance of non-technical factors to attitudes on technical issues will be demonstrated in the next section by summarizing results of two empirical studies.

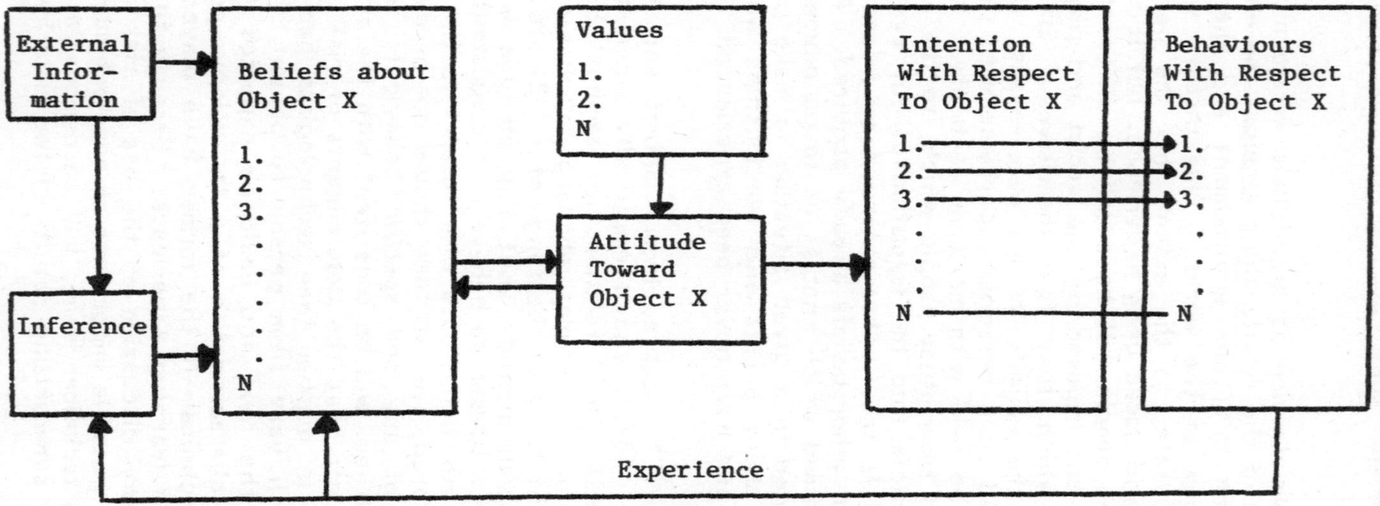

Figure 1. The Formation of Beliefs and Their Relation to Attitude and Behavior. (Adapted from Fishbein and Ajzen, 1975).

Two Empirical Demonstrations

Both studies to be summarized here used Fishbein's attitude model (Fishbein and Ajzen, 1975) which allows attitude (risk perception if so defined) to be measured as a function of its underlying beliefs and values. This model, which has had extensive empirical verification in a variety of subject areas, is of the expectancy value type and assumes that attitude can be estimated by weighting belief strength by attribute evaluation and summing the products over the salient beliefs. An independent, direct measure of the same attitude is obtained to ensure, through correlation of indirect and direct measures, that the model has provided a satisfactory estimate of attitude.

Public Respondents

The respondents in the first study (Otway and Fishbein, 1977; Otway, et al, 1978) were a stratified sample of 224 members of the Austrian public, whose attitudes with respect to the use of five types of energy systems were elicited in early 1977. The sample was not intended to be representative of the Austrian population but was a stratified sample, controlling for geographical location (Vienna, provincial capital, and rural), sex, age, and education level. This sample size was sufficient to explore the effects of demographic variables upon attitudes while still staying within the financial resources of the project. (In the event, sex was the only demographic variable of significance, i.e. women were found to be significantly less favourable than men in their attitudes toward the use of nuclear energy.)

The attitude distributions were found (Thomas and Otway, 1980b) to be of three types: highly favourable for hydro and solar; moderately favourable for coal and oil; and tri-modal (partially due to end-of-scale effects) for nuclear energy; all attitudes were elicited with respect to their underlying beliefs and values. Because of the interesting distribution of the attitudes toward nuclear energy, their underlying beliefs were looked at in greater depth.

Factor analysis[2] was used to group the most highly intercorrelated belief items, revealing four independent types of issue (factors) to underlie public perceptions on this topic:[3] beliefs about the economic and technical benefits (e.g., providing good economic value, leading to industrial development); beliefs about environmental and physical risks (e.g., air and water pollution); an "anxiety"

Table 1. Contributions to Attitude: Public Sample

Dimension	Attitude Contribution	
	PRO Group	CON Group*
Technical/Economic Benefits	3.4	0.2
Environmental/Physical Risks	1.8	-1.4
Psychological Aspects	-1.6	-6.4
Socio-Political Implications	-1.2	-3.2

*All PRO/CON differences significant at $p < 0.01$ (student t test)

factor comprising beliefs of psychological significance (e.g. consent, control, catastrophic consequences, delayed effects); and beliefs about the social and political implications of the technology (e.g., dependency upon small expert groups, need for special police powers, possibility of mis-use by terrorists). A comparison of the contributions made by each dimension (scale range +9 to -9) to the attitudes of the 50 people most *for* the use of nuclear energy and the 50 people most *against* is shown in Table 1[4] (detailed information on belief and value systems is reported in Otway and Fishbein, 1977; Otway et al, 1978).

These findings demonstrate the complexity of attitudes. People perceived risks and benefits independently rather than as lying along a single axis, as might be inferred from the general notion of cost-benefit analysis. Further, they differentiated amongst different types of risk: for example, one could believe that a technology would lead to socially unacceptable conditions without necessarily believing that it would cause environmental risks. In this study, the largest contributions to the attitudes of the Pro Group were made by the two factors of benefits and environmental risks. In contrast, psychological and socio-political aspects dominated the attitudes of the Con Group.

Policy Makers as Respondents

The second study (Thomas et al, 1980a) used the same questionnaire and procedure to measure the attitudes of policy makers in the Austrian Energy Ministry. The sample of policy makers consisted of 40 senior civil servants specializing in energy matters; 34 of the respondents were male, 6 were female. This group of 40 people represented virtually all of the ministry staff in this category who were in duty at the time of the survey; only one person refused to participate. About five weeks after the respondents had completed the questionnaire for the first time, expressing their personal points of view, they were randomly assigned to one of the two role-play subgroups (i.e., playing the role of a typical Austrian citizen in favor of or against the use of nuclear energy) to obtain estimates of the policy makers' perceptions of the beliefs and attitudes of members of the public. Only 35 of the original group of 40 were available for the role-play part of the study (N=17 for the PRO-role, and N=18 for the CON-role). This experimental design allowed the policy makers' own attitudes to be compared to those of the general public and also made it possible to test the accuracy of their perceptions of particular public positions.

Table 2. Contributions to Attitude: Comparison of Public and Policy Makers

Dimension	Attitude Contribution	
	Policy Makers (n=40)	Total Public Sample (n=224)
Technical/Economic Benefits	1.6	1.8
Environmental/Physical Risks	1.8	0.3**
Psychological Aspects	-0.4	-3.8**
Socio-Political Implications	-1.8	-2.3
Overall Attitude	+1.2	-3.9**

**Difference significant at $p < 0.01$ (student t test)

Table 3. Contributions to Attitude: Accuracy of Policy Makers' Role-Play Responses

Dimension		Attitude Contribution	
		Public	Policy Makers In Role Play
Technical/Economic Benefits	PRO	3.4	3.3
	CON	0.2	-0.2
Environmental/Physical Risks	PRO	1.8	2.2
	CON	-1.4	-1.7
Psychological Aspects	PRO	-1.6	1.3**
	CON	-6.4	-5.2**
Socio-Political Implications	PRO	-1.2	-0.2
	CON	-3.2	-3.2

**Differences significant at $p < 0.01$ (student t test)

Overall the policy makers' attitude toward the use of nuclear energy was found to be +1.2 compared to -3.9 for the total public sample, significant at $p < 0.01$. (The maximum scale range was +36 to -36.) Table 2[5] shows the contributions made to attitude by each of the four underlying dimensions for the total public sample and the total policy makers sample.

The underlying reasons for this significant difference in attitudes were primarily: (1) that the policy makers were more certain than the public that the use of nuclear energy would not lead to environmental and health and safety risks; and (2) that the public found a stronger association with less technical aspects of psychological significance, such as consent, control, etc.

In the next part of this experiment the policy makers were asked to respond in the role of a typical member of the public who was Pro or Con the use of nuclear energy. The overall accuracy of this role play, on each of the four dimensions, can be seen in Table 3.

Although the policy makers' overall role-play responses were quite accurate, it was only on a non-technical dimension (psychological aspects) where they significantly underestimated the negative contributions made to both Pro and Con public attitudes.

Of course the results summarized here are only valid for the particular samples reported, at the time the samples were taken, and there is no wish to try to generalize from the specific results. They were presented simply to demonstrate the role non-technical issues can play on ostensibly technical topics in differentiating between the attitudes of public groups as well as between the public and policy maker's own attitudes. And, perhaps more important, that technically trained policy makers may experience difficulty in appreciating the significance of non-technical issues to public attitudes on questions such as energy planning. The reader interested in other approaches to measuring risk perception and results of empirical applications is referred to the work of the Decision Research group (Fischhoff, 1978b; Slovic et al, 1979).

The Use of Risk Analyses

The introduction referred to three types of actors who have become involved in the evolution of regulatory criteria which, directly or indirectly, specify societal risk-taking: the regulator, the technology-sponsor, and public groups.[6]

The empirical results just summarized suggest that they are not likely to share common values and beliefs,[7] consequently they each have different definitions of risk and different criteria for judging its acceptability. Further, each actor has a different role and responsibilities and must operate within a different set of constraints. The following sections will discuss the uses each actor might have for risk analyses in the light of his own particular role, responsibilities and constraints.

The Regulator

One of the regulator's basic statutory objectives is to provide regulations that will ensure an adequate degree of public protection. Since "adequate" cannot be rigorously defined, this objective might be reflected in a very general concern that his regulations find a broad base of support--a concern related in the longer term to more mundane issues of organizational and personal survival. The search for regulatory acceptance may be expressed as a strong desire for consistency amongst policy goals and regulations, and as a fear of alienating politically powerful individuals or groups while, at the same time, avoiding the image of being indifferent to public demands for protection.

Quantitative risk estimation results can be useful for meeting only the most obvious statutory objective by providing supporting evidence, but never proof (Polanyi, 1958; Majone, 1980), that anticipated public risk exposures are below some "maximum-tolerable limit" of risk. This "maximum tolerable" risk limit might even be derived through statistical analysis of existing levels of socially acceptable risk, although the numerical value of this upper risk limit will not be constant but will depend on the specific decision context and its relationship to, for example, national priorities.

However, even the comparison of estimated levels of the new risk with the "maximum tolerable" criterium is not straight forward. For example, a new risk characterized by a low expected value, but with large uncertainties attached to it, might well be judged less acceptable than another risk with a higher expected value where the uncertainty of the estimate has been made small through experience; thus, although both risks may satisfy the upper limit criterion, the risk with the higher expected value might be accepted and the lower risk rejected. Another factor complicating such comparisons is that some risks are characterized by a low probability of high consequence accidents, while others are not; further, some risks have immediate effects while others are delayed in time or even taken by future generations; and so on.

Thus, contrary to the suggestions made by Rothschild (1978) and others (Okrent, 1980), the comparison of risk estimates with statistics reflecting social experience of existing risks can provide useful, but never sufficient, information to judge the acceptability of the new risk. Risks meeting this criterion may still not be accepted by public groups. On the other hand, evidence that a new risk (or its uncertainty) is high compared to existing risks could well be sufficient to cause the regulator, in view of his basic interests in public protection, to demand rejection, or re-design, of the technology. (That this is not always even sufficient information to provide a consensus for risk rejection may be seen in the debate in the USA about the ban of artificial sweeteners.)

Technical risk studies might be useful to the regulator, and sometimes even necessary, in order to provide concrete assurance that risks are being taken seriously, but alone they can never provide an adequate basis for policy formation.

The regulator's goal of regulatory acceptability implies that, in some as yet unspecified way, he will be responsive to the preferences and beliefs of the affected publics and the technology-sponsor. Earlier in this paper results of surveys were presented which permitted members of the public to express themselves in a structured format with respect to policy options. This raises the question of what role surveys can, or should play in the formation of policy.

Knowledge of beliefs and values can be used to predict the behaviour of social groups with respect to different policy options (Fishbein and Ajzen, 1975), but the survey results will be relevant only to the precise question posed (assuming the questionnaire has been adequately designed). For example, there is no reason to expect that the attitude toward *voting* in an energy referendum (Bowman et al, 1978) would relate closely to attitudes toward the energy systems themselves. This means that, in principle, there are an infinite number of attitude objects and the policy maker has no basis for extrapolating survey results from one attitude object to another. Further, the results are perishable with time so, once measured, they may not be valid for long--especially on issues which are new or volatile.

Policy makers could, in principle, ask then for attitude measures relevant to some very specific policy choice with the idea of selecting the option most popular with the affected publics. However, the decision maker who relied on survey results would almost certainly be charged with abnegation of responsibility by those with economic or professional interests in the particular technology, not to mention claims of disenfranchisement by the electorate. And, regardless of the competence of attitude analyses, it seems likely that their objectivity and reliability would be questioned: one can imagine the same interminable and dreary debates that have surrounded technical risk studies being reenacted, this time with conflicting social scientists in the starring roles.

Again, analogous to risk estimation results, studies of risk attitudes can provide useful background information for policy formation but, of themselves, cannot dictate policy. Technical questions of survey reliability aside (Fischhoff et al, 1979), the real value of studies which analyze attitudes and their underlying beliefs and values may be to demonstrate to policy makers and technology-sponsors the complexity of public thinking on policy issues.

The Technology-Sponsor

The technology-sponsor must comply with regulations, including possible risk criteria, and, at the same time, satisfy product-related economic objectives. But, regardless of the investment made in risk reduction, there will always be a "residual risk" that cannot be reduced to zero because real equipment, real operators, and real designers are not perfect.

These technical and human realities, coupled with economic constraints, define the "minimum feasible" level of residual risk that the technology-sponsor can achieve. Technical risk studies can help him to find an economically efficient way to keep the "minimum-feasible" risk level below the regulator's "maximum tolerable" risk limit, and, in general, to aid in understanding and designing his system. However, in the absence of economic sanctions such as effluent taxes, the technology sponsor has little incentive to reduce risks below the maximum allowed by law. If political pressures for risk reduction force actual risks to approach or go below the "minimum feasible" level the technology-sponsor's market position may begin to erode, forcing him to withdraw from the activity, to seek re-negotiation of regulatory criteria or, perhaps, even to resort to subterfuge.

There are often calls made for "balanced risk reduction" on a national level, based on the assertion that efficient use of society's limited resources requires their allocation such that the marginal cost per life saved is roughly constant for all technologically based activities. These calls are coupled with the observation that risk studies show safety levels to vary widely from one activity to the next, and that the additional expenditures required to "save" one more "statistical life" vary even more. Although this argument seems quite reasonable on the surface, decisions on programmes which affect public safety are often more influenced by political considerations (eg, regional distribution of funds, single-interest lobbies) than by the dry risk numbers; further, politics aside, direct distributional mechanisms to allocate funds amongst different risk reduction opportunities do not exist. Thus the use of technical risk studies to support reduction in safety costs for a specific technology may be viewed by some with a certain amount of skepticism, seeing the calculations as intended to serve particular economic interests instead of the public good.

The Public

The objectives of the larger public are more complex, and sometimes conflicting. Viewed in the narrow context of risk, the public may want to enjoy the benefits of technology while, at the same time, being free of its risks--or at least free of anxiety about risk.

As demonstrated earlier, public attitudes toward technological risks are based not only on "objective" risk and benefit data but also can incorporate a variety of psychological and social value issues. Because of this, and the basic stability of attitudes once formed, it has been argued elsewhere (Otway, 1980) that public attitudes are not likely to be responsive to the information provided by risk studies (at least they are not likely to influence people in the direction of risk acceptance; however, a study which appears to have reasonable scientific credentials could well influence the public to reject a risk). Aside from a few interest groups who have carried out their own risk analyses as a basis to question the results of officially sponsored studies, the general public is not likely to have much interest in the results of quantitative risk analysis -- at least this has been the pattern observed in the public response (in several countries) to estimates of nuclear energy risks.

Concluding Comments

These three actor types each bring their own values and beliefs into a negotiating process which, in effect, determines the regulatory conditions under which a technology can be accepted. Technologies are, and always have been, judged on the basis of a broad range of political, social, economic, and technical criteria--risk is just one issue amongst many. Consistent with this observation, we have argued that risk analyses can sometimes aid the regulatory process by supplying relevant background information; but if analysts and policy makers are unaware of the inherent limitations to analysis posed by the risk framework they might be led to interpret this information as scientific "proof" sufficient to support a particular policy (Ravetz, 1971). This would be tantamount to the translation of inexact estimates into clear policy decisions which, however "correct" from a narrow technical perspective, imply the exclusion of some actors from the decision-making process, thereby further aggravating the conflicts that risk analysis was intended to resolve.

Notes

[1]Any opinions expressed are solely those of the author. Paper written in collaboration with the FAST Programme of the Commission of the European Communities.

[2]Factor analysis is a generic term for a set of linear, parametric statistical methods which identify the minimum number of independent dimensions needed to account for the variance in a larger set of intercorrelated variables. The method used here was that of principal components analysis, followed by varimax rotation. This technique produces underlying dimensions which are independent, i.e., orthogonal factors.

[3]This four factor solution accounted for 49% of the variance in the data (factor eigenvalues 6.04, 5.17, 4.03, and 4.01).

[4]The five attributes which loaded the highest on each of the four belief dimensions were used to calculate "factor-summaries" representative of each dimension. In each case the five belief strengths were summed, as were the corresponding attribute evaluations. These two sums were then multiplied in line with the attitude model used, to give an index of the contribution of that belief to overall attitude. It is these summaries of attitude contribution that

are shown in Table 1. To test the validity of reducing the 39 original attributes to 20 attributes (5 per dimension) an estimate of attitude based on a sum of these four factor-summary products was correlated with the direct (semantic differential) measure of attitude. The Pearson correlation coefficient was r=0.66, as compared with r=0.63 when all 39 attributes were used.

[5]For the policy makers' sample the correlation between the direct measure of attitude and the belief-based measure, using all 39 attributes, was 0.89. While it would have been desirable to perform a factor analysis of the policy makers' belief scores, the number of respondents (n=40) was too small to obtain meaningful results for a set of 39 beliefs. Therefore the factor structure obtained for the public sample was also used to summarize the policy makers' data; after calculating the "factor summaries" (by the same procedure used for Table 1) the correlation coefficient between the two attitude measures was found to be 0.85, thus indicating the validity of using only 20 beliefs.

[6]In reality there are several actors in each category, eg, corporate shareholders, suppliers, sub-contractors, labour unions, lending institutions, local governments, professional societies.

[7]A simplification: For example, technical experts in each category might have rather similar values and beliefs while, in contrast, each category might include groups having fundamentally different ideologies, but united by filling similar roles.

References

Ajzen, I. and M. Fishbein (1977), *Psych. Bull., 84,* 888.

Bowman, C. and M. Fishbein, H.J. Otway, and K. Thomas (1978), *The Prediction of Voting Behavior in a Nuclear Energy Referendum.* Laxenburg, Austria: Int'l. Institute for Applied Systems Analysis.

Farmer, F.R. (1967), *Nuclear Safety, 8,* 539.

Fishbein, M. and I. Ajzen (1975). *Attitude, Belief, Intention and Behavior: An Introduction to Theory and Research.* Reading, PA: Addison-Wesley.

Fischhoff, B. (1978a), *Policy Science, 8,* 177.

Fischhoff, B. (1978b), *Policy Science, 9,* 127.

Fischhoff, B., P. Slovic, S. Lichtenstein (1979). "Knowing What You Want: Measuring Labile Values." *Cognitive Processes in Choice and Decision Behavior.* (Ed.) T. Wallsken, Erlbaum.

Holden, J. Jr. (1966), *Pollution Control as Bargaining Process--An Essay on Regulatory Decision Making.* Ithaca, NY: Cornell University Press.

Inhaber, H. (1978), "Risks of Energy Production," Canadian Atomic Energy Commission Report.

Kates, R.W. (1976), "Risk Assessment of Environmental Hazard," *Scope.*

Lagadac, P. (1977), "Developpement, Environnement et Politique vis-a-vis du Risque," *Rapport D 1680977,* Paris: Ecole Polytechnique.

Majone, G. (1975), "On the Logic of Standard Setting in Health and Related Fields," *Systems Analysis of Health Planning.* (Eds.) N. Bailey and M. Thompson, No. Holland.

Masone, G. and E.S. Quade (Eds.) (1980), *Pitfalls of Analysis.* UK: Wiley.

Nuclear Regulatory Commission (1975). *US Reactor Safety Study,* Wash-1400 (NuReg-75/014).

Okrent, D. (1980), *Science, 208,* 372.

Otway, H.J. et al (1975), *Revealed Preferences: Comments on The Starr Risk-Benefit Relationships.* Laxenburg, Austria: Int'l. Institute for Applied Systems Analysis, RM-75-5.

Otway, H.J. and P.D. Pahner (1976). *Futures, 8,* 122.

Otway, H.J. and M. Fishbein (1977), *Public Attitudes and Decision Making.* Laxenburg, Austria: Int'l Institute for Applied Systems Analysis. RM-77-54.

Otway, H.J., D. Maurer, and K. Thomas (1978), *Futures, 10,* 109.

Otway, H.J. (1980), "Risk Perception: A Psychological Perspective". *Technological Risk: Its Perception and Handling in the European Community.* (Eds.) M.

Dierks, S. Edwards, and R. Coppock. Cambridge, Mass.: Oelgeschlager, Gunn & Hain

Polanyi, M. (1958). *Personal Knowledge.* Chicago: University of Chicago Press.

Ravetz, J.J., (1971) *Scientific Knowledge and its Social Problems.* Oxford: Clarendon Press.

Rowe, W.D. (1977). *An Anatomy of Risk.* New York: Wiley.

Rothschild, Lord (1978), *Risk.* London: British Broadcasting Corp.

Slovic, P., B. Fischhoff, and S. Lichtenstein (1979), *Environment, 21,* 14.

Starr, C. (1964), *Nuclear Safety, 5,* 325.

Starr, C. (1969), *Science, 165,* 1232.

Thomas, K., E. Swaton, M. Fishbein, and H.J. Otway (1980a), *Nuclear Energy: The Accuracy of Policy Makers Perceptions of Public Beliefs.* Laxenburg, Austria: Int'l. Institute for Applied Systems Analysis. RR-80-18. Also published in *Behavioral Science,* 25, 332 (1980).

Thomas, K. and H.J. Otway (1980b). "Public Perceptions of Energy Systems Risks: Some Policy Implications," *Progress in Resource Management and Environmental Planning, Vol. II.* (Eds.) T. O'Riordan and R.K. Turner, Wiley.

Weinberg, A.M. (1972), *Minerva, 10,* 209.

Seymour Warkov

7. Attitudes Toward the Future: Their Impact on Present Decisions

Abstract

Following an overview of research on the impact of future orientations on educational and occupational attainment (and aspirations), delinquency, family planning and other behaviors, the paper assesses available studies of natural resource consumption, individual and household energy consumption and conservation, and the like for evidence of a time-orientation effect. The age relationship documented in these studies is considered in terms of implicit temporal perspectives. Data from the author's household survey of solar adopters and near-adopters are utilized to test a presumptive relationship between future orientation and household decision making concerning solar hot water technology. Implications for policy research on natural resource consumption are discussed in a concluding note.

Introduction

The study of time perspective (including future orientations) has produced a substantial literature based on social and behavioral theory and empirical research. Leonard Doob's 1971 synthesis and integration of this literature draws upon a bibliography exceeding 800 items (Doob, 1971). In this presentation I wish to consider selected empirical studies on orientations toward the future and decisions concerning energy conservation. This brief overview is followed by a case-study that draws upon a Spring, 1979, telephone interview survey of factors affecting household adoption of solar hot water technology. Future orientations are reflected in perceptions of public and private benefits associated with solar technology and in perceptions of diminishing fossil fuel supplies. These perceptions are hypothesized to operate as one set of conditions facilitating the conversion of strong interest in solar into a tangible investment decision (Warkov, 1979; Warkov and Meyer, 1982).

Time perspectives, including future orientations, are an important dimension of cognition. By time perspective we mean... "the individual's cognitions concerning the content, placement and unfolding of relevant events in his past, present and future" (Lamm et al, 1976). Social scientists have postulated a relationship between time perspective, especially future orientation, and traditionalism/modernism. According to Kluckhohn and Murray, Texans and Mormons tend to be future oriented, while the Zuni and Navaho tend to be oriented to the past but also emphasize the future more than the present (Kluckhohn and Strodtbeck, 1961). These findings are employed on behalf of the proposition that a person's social behavior and time perspective are shaped by his sociocultural setting.

Given the universality of social stratification in human society, power relations between groups and individuals can affect time perspectives. If Africans are less future-oriented than their white counterparts (Doob, 1971), these differences can be attributed to social structure, inequality, and differential access to social and material resources. By the same token social and behavioral scientists aver that deferred gratification (i.e., the ability to delay rewards), achievement motivation and future time perspectives are interrelated. Future orientations shape educational and occupational attainment (Duncan et al, 1976). Furthermore, future orientations allegedly differentiate middle class and working class culture. And individual attitudes, feelings and perceptions toward the future differentiate personality types as well as cultural systems (Doob, 1971).

Future expectations occupy a significant place in economic theories seeking to explain human behavior. For example, the commodity markets exemplify the key role of time perspective: since all commodity trading hinges on future delivery, expectations concerning prospects for supply and demand entirely determine current behavior of economic actors. Or consider the economics of environmental protection: in evaluating the long-term gains as well as the short-term and long-run impacts of projects requiring capital outlays, a cost/benefit analysis offers explicit judgments about the probable benefits based on a forecast for each year of the life of the project (Thompson, 1973).

Turning to relevant social science research on energy conservation and environmental orientation, the National

Opinion Research Center's study of household responses to the 1973-1974 oil embargo notes that expectations are derived from past experience, appraisals of current circumstances, and "anticipation of future events" (Murray et al, 1974). This longitudinal survey concluded that short-term expectations are affected by exposure to shortages and do determine conservation behavior. "Longer term (expectations) are insensitive to recent experiences of shortages, relatively stable over time and unrelated to evaluations of the energy shortage and conservation behaviors" (Murray et al, 1974). Even the link between short-term expectations and conservation behavior, I would argue, depends on belief in a genuine energy problem and acceptance of sacrifice or inconvenience imposed by various conservation measures. An October, 1979, state-wide survey of Connecticut residents found that a majority consider the long-term energy problem to be real (51%), consider current problems "just a scheme by the oil companies to increase their profits" (67%), and expect "long gas lines again in the next several months" (60%). However, measures to reduce fuel consumption gain support from a minority: only 1 in 5 endorse a halt to all new highway construction in the State, and less than a majority (4 in 10) support the new speeding law requiring mandatory appearance in court if ticketed for exceeding the 55 mph limit. The more stringent the proposed conservation measure the less support offered by the public, commitment to general principles of energy conservation notwithstanding (Connecticut Poll, 1979).

An assessment of the impact of future orientations on current conservation behavior must also accord special attention to age groups and to the age structure of our society. A recent overview of determinants of energy conservation concluded: "Age is the only sociodemographic characteristic that is closely related to conservation actions" (Olsen, 1978). At the same time, a half dozen surveys indicate that age is a stronger predictor than education of environmental orientations and attitudes. Younger respondents score higher on environmental concern, awareness of environmental problems, attitudes toward pollution, support for environmental reform, and the like (Buttel and Flinn, 1974; Constantini and Hunt, 1972; Dillman and Christenson, 1972; Tognacci et al, 1972). In brief, younger Americans report a greater propsensity to conserve energy and younger Americans are more extensively committed to environmentalism. On the other hand, the bulk of the empirical evidence to date indicates little relationship between attitudes and behavior in the domain of energy conservation (Milstein, 1978; Peelman and Warren, 1977). Does this imply that the young display the familiar human failing "Twixt the cup and the lip"? Fundamental political and economic decision making affecting aggregate energy demand and environmental amelioration is not especially the domain of Americans born since 1945.

Distinctive age group differences that are linear are reported in a national survey for Resources For the Future: 7 in 10 respondents under age 24 were designated as supporters of environmental protection at any cost; among their counterparts aged 65 and older, only 3 in 10 were so classified (Mitchell, 1978). Presumably younger respondents also are more sensitive to the long-run implications of resource scarcity. Another example: the survey of Connecticut households found predictable age-specific relationships with six survey items touching on the "hard path" (eg. nuclear) as an alternative to fossil fuels (Connecticut Poll, 1979). The young were more likely to oppose building new nuclear power plants, including Millstone III in Connecticut, to consider a sequel to Three Mile Island a real possibility in the State, to reject the notion that the risks of nuclear have been exaggerated, etc.

An age relationship derived from a one time sample is subject to problems of interpretation that are familiar to all survey analysts. Is it maturation (aging)? A generational effect reflecting exposure to unique historical events that shape age-group political consciousness? Or perhaps a cohort effect (Glenn, 1977)? Younger Americans may be especially oriented towards prospective shortages in energy resources, a disposition that is particularly congruent with conservation behavior. For example, in response to the survey item, "We will probably have long gas lines again the next several months" 7 in 10 Connecticut respondents under age 30 agreed; among their counterparts 68 years and over, less than half (46%) agreed. One well established conservation strategy in response to gasoline shortages would be adherence to 55 mile per hour speed limit. Yet, the young (under 30) were less likely than the old (over 60) to approve the following statement: "There is a new law in Connecticut that anyone caught going over 55 has to appear in traffic court instead of just mailing in a fine." (34% vs. 56% approving). For that matter, even the relatively benign proposal to provide a special lane for car pools during commuting hours was less agreeable to younger respondents (Connecticut Poll, 1979). In brief, expectations of near-term fuel shortages did not generate distinctive support among younger respondents for measures fostering fuel conservation. More research is required on age group, future expectations and conservation behavior if we are to unravel the effects of aging, age cohort, and time period on patterns of resource consumption. My brief overview of this issue points to a complex pattern of relationships that defies simple causal modelling.

The Decision to Buy Household Solar

In the following section of my presentation, I review my own work on household decision making with respect to the acquisition of domestic solar hot water systems and pay special attention to the possibility that future expectations affected that decision. The data are drawn from a two year study of the HUD Solar Hot Water Program in the State of Connecticut.

In Spring, 1977, the mass media disseminated information about the availability of 750 four hundred dollar grants for home owners who meet eligibility requirements for solar hot water systems. By September, 1977, some 2200 Connecticut households contacted State energy officials administering the program for additional information; over 900 completed one page application forms and 750 received conditional approval subject to various program requirements. By January 1978, follow up contacts determined that *550* were still pursuing the grant; as of June 1978, only *150* households had provided documentation required to qualify for this subsidy. Applicants dropping out of the program were replaced by households on the wait list. Widespread defection prompted the Northeast Solar Energy Center to commission a household telephone interview survey of program applicants. During Spring 1979 a random sample of 215 households were contacted to acquire systematic information about factors contributing to this decision. Interviews were completed with some 82 percent of this sample. In each instance contacts were made with the household member signing the application form. A key finding was the following: 61 families had purchased solar hot water systems as of May 1979; 121 families did not acquire solar systems despite their initial interest in the program.

Selected correlates of solar adoption are displayed in Table 1. A complete description of all variables employed in the analysis to predict solar adoption is reported elsewhere (Warkov, 1979). One additional variable was added for this paper: it is the response to the survey item, "Many factors have been mentioned as causes of energy shortages... The world is running out of fossil fuel supplies." Among solar adopters, 7 in 10 agreed with that statement; among solar non-adopters less than half (46%) did likewise.

Table 1. Description of Variables and Zero-Order Correlations

Variable	Mean	Standard Deviation	Unadjusted N	Zero-Order Correlation with SOLUSER
1. ENCOURIN	3.55	2.99	159	.323
2. SOLPRBEN	4.78	2.23	165	.284
3. ROOFIN	2.04	.91	176	.193
4. SOLSAVIN	5.19	1.23	178	.113
5. SOLINSUR	4.26	1.59	178	-.055
6. SHORT	2.28	.89	175	.159
7. SOLUSER	1.32	.47	178	-----

The six variables in this table are:

1. *Encouragement index* (ENCOURIN) is based on the series of items concerning communications with various "change agents." (Contact *and* encouragement = l; all others = 0). For example, Talked to and was encouraged to purchase solar by the solar dealer, solar engineer, friends, etc.

2. *Roof index* (ROOFIN) is based on 3 items concerning shade (never shaded = 1; all other = 0); southern exposure (yes = 1; no = 0); and rating of layout of roof (very suitable = 1; all other = 0).

3. *Private benefits of solar* (SOLPRBEN) is based on four items from a battery concerning advantages associated with solar systems (major advantage, adds to resale value of home = 2; minor advantage = 1; no advantage = 0; major advantage, infrequent, and easy maintenance = 2; minor advantage = 1; none = 0; do-it-yourself appeal: major = 2; minor = 1; no advantage = 0; and service by local businessman: major = 2; minor = 1; no advantage = 0).

4. *Savings* (SOLSAVIN) associated with solar, based on 3 items: major advantage in fuel savings = 2; minor = 1; none = 0. "Insurance against rising fuel prices," and "it will eventually save money" were the second and third items.

5. *Protection* (SOLINSUR) based on 3 items concerning advantages associated with energy independence, preserve natural resources, and protection against outages. These items were scaled in identical fashion.

6. *Fossil fuel depletion* (SHORT) based on an item concerning global depletion of fossil fuel supplies (agree = 1; disagree or don't know = 0).

An additional transformation was performed because complete information was not always available for every variable or index. In each instance, the mean score of the population was substituted to preserve the case base. The procedure slightly depressed the zero-order correlations between the six "independent" variables and the dependent variable:

Table 2. Intercorrelations Among Four Predictor Variables and Adoption of Solar (N=178 Households)*

	SOLUSER	ENCOURIN	SOLPRBEN	ROOFIN	SHORT
SOLUSER	-	323	284	193	159
ENCOURIN		-	306	050	-089
SOLPRBEN			-	090	087
ROOFIN				-	002
SHORT					-

*Decimal points of correlation coefficients are omitted.

Table 3. Regression Estimates of Equation For Adopting Household Solar, Spring, 1979, By HUD Program Entrants, Fall, 1977

	Predictor Variables			
	ENCOURIN	SOLPRBEN	SHORT	ROOFIN
B	.052	.036	.086	.081
(SE)	.015	.015	.036	.035
Beta	.242	.168	.165	.158
F	11.1*	5.3**	5.7*	5.3**

$R^2 = .171$ *$p < .001$ **$p < .01$

7. *Solar user* (SOLUSER): household adopted solar = 1; no = 0.

Table 1 displays the mean and standard deviation for each variable, the case base prior to adjustment for non-responses and the zero-order correlation with household solar adoption. A correlation of .12 ($p < .05$) or higher would be considered statistically significant, but correlations of this magnitude "explain" very little. A preliminary assessment of these correlations suggests that the social environment of prospective adopters as indexed by the *volume* of encouragement they received from significant actors, perception of solar system advantages that could be classified as "private" rather than "public" benefits, the configuration of the roof and, finally, perception of eventual global depletion of fossil fuels comprise the four dimensions of the adoption process for which empirical verification might be possible on the basis of these results. On the other hand, the measures tapping social benefits in the form of preservation of natural resources, national independence from OPEC and the like shows very little effect ($r = -.05$).

More surprising, a measure reflecting private economic benefits (fuel savings, insurance against rising fuel prices, eventually save money) did not significantly correlate with household solar adoption ($r = .11$).

Table 2 and Table 3 display the correlation matrix and the results of a multiple regression analysis representing our "best" set of predictors of household solar adoption. The beta values for the measures of encouragement to purchase solar (.236) and perception of private benefits of solar (.204) are especially noteworthy. Furthermore, these two variates are related ($r = .31$), but the study design (one-time sample survey of households) and data on hand preclude any statement about causal direction, i.e., do households receiving much encouragement to purchase solar then perceive private benefits, or do households perceiving private benefits associated with solar engage in a high volume of communication concerning solar that proves to be supportive? When both conditions are present, HUD applicants are more likely to translate initial interest into concrete behavior.

The beta value for the variate concerning global fossil fuel depletion (.181) is in accord with formulations of future expectations discussed earlier. Note that this item is uncorrelated with measures of communication behavior or a judgment that solar systems confer private non-economic benefits to the household. Therefore it appears that the perception of dimishing fossil fuels supplies contributing to energy shortages facilitates the purchase of solar technology apart from the amount of encouragement reported by the respondent and apart from other benefits derived from solar systems reported by respondents.

Another predictor variable consists of the roof index (b = .135). The results are self evident: households residing in dwellings with a Southern exposure, a roof that is never shaded, and a roof "lay out" deemed very suitable for solar are more likely to acquire the technology than households not meeting these conditions. Clearly, a significant "barrier" to adoption, but only one of many.

In brief, households initially interested in receiving a HUD grant to install solar water systems were more likely to acquire this technology when energy shortages were linked to a perception of declining world fossil fuel supplies. While the distinction between short-term and long-term expectations is blurred in this instance, it is fair to assume the Connecticut homeowners relying on imported heating oil were sensitized to the prospects of supply availability. Our findings offer support for the proposition that future orientations can influence conservation behavior as indicated above.

Discussion and Concluding Comments

Because my assignment concerns the contribution of future orientations to current conservation behavior, I want to consider the significance of these results. As of Spring, 1979, homeowners interested in solar were likely to acquire this technology if future orientations were based on a perception of fossil fuel depletion, i.e., fear that some day the oil spigot will run dry. On the other hand, an index based on implicit appeals to meet one's obligations to society and to future generations, i.e., preserve natural resources, foster independence from oil supplying nations, etc., via solar systems generated non-significant effects. As for benefits to prospective solar users based on "insurance against rising fuel prices", "will eventually save money", etc., again we found trivial effects with regard to solar adoption. At this stage of solar commercialization it is possible that the emphasis on savings is premature. Another consideration concerns the timing of these telephone interviews (i.e., March, April, 1979). Homeowners in the Northeast paying 65 cents or so for a gallon of heating oil in Spring, 1979, did not perceive the savings associated with solar; homeowners paying an expected 90 cents to one dollar per gallon during Winter, 1980, may see matters differently. Not to be overlooked, moreover, is the possibility that the experience of owning a solar collector resulted in a perception that the technology did not at the time (Spring 1979) afford an advantage in near-term savings.

Reflecting on conditions that promote conservation measures when the present generation will not directly enjoy the benefits of renunciation (conservation), Leonard Doob (1971) specifies: first, an appeal to "future generations", that is, unalloyed altruism; second, an appeal for sacrifice linked to gratitude expressed by the beneficiaries now or in the conservor's old age; and three, an appeal to conserve based on gratitude to past generations for *their* sacrifices, in turn obliging the present generation to conserve on behalf of the future. Doob concludes that man does exercise his capacities for renunciation on behalf of future generations "...but he exercises them reluctantly and then only when some benefits, frequently only of a spiritual nature, occur to him in the present" (Doob, 1971).

Many benefits of conservation, to be sure, are not remote but immediate. In this context, Stobaugh and Yergin recently argued on behalf of appeals to self interest rather than appeals based on renunciation and moral principle (Stobaugh and Yergin, 1979). Their substantive proposals are familiar ones: larger incentives in the form of tax credits, loans, and grants to achieve an immediate reduction in U.S. dependence on imported petroleum. My own work on "solar pioneers", especially results reported here suggests that an appeal based on *fear* may be required to supplement the economic and moral incentives proposed above. Continuing U.S. dependency on Persian Gulf oil supplies is hardly reassuring in light of the Iranian revolution, the assassination of Egypt's president, Anwar Sadat, and other indicators of chronic regional instability. These developments underscore the need now, as in 1973, for major conservation efforts and public investments in compatible alternate energy resources.

References

Buttel, F.H. and W.L. Flinn (1974), "The Structure of Support for the Environmental Movement," *Rural Sociology, 39*, 56-59.

Connecticut Poll (1979), *CONNPOLL #2*. Social Science Data Center: University of Connecticut.

Constantini, E. and K. Hunt (1972), "Environmental Concern and Lake Tahoe: A Study of Elite Perceptions, Backgrounds, and Attitudes," *Environment and Behavior*, *4*, 209-242.

Dillman, D.A. and J.A. Christenson (1972), "The Public Value for Pollution Control," *Social Behavior, Natural Resources, and the Environment*. (Eds), W.R. Burch et al. New York: Harper and Row.

Doob, L.W. (1971), *Patterning in Time*. New Haven and London: Yale University Press.

Duncan, O.D., D.L. Featherman and B. Duncan (1972). *Socioeconomic Background and Achievement*. New York: Seminar Press.

Glenn, N.D. (1977), *Cohort Analysis*. Beverly Hills and London: Sage Publications.

Kluckhohn, F.R. and F.L. Strodtbeck (1961), *Variations in Value Orientations*. Evanston: Illinois: Row, Peterson.

Lamm, H., R.W. Schmidt and G. Trommsdorff (1976), "Sex and Social Class as Determinants of Future Orientation (Time Perspective) in Adolescents," *J. Pers and Soc. Psych.*, *34*, 317.

Milstein, J.S. (1978), "How Consumers Feel About Energy: Attitudes and Behavior During Winter and Spring 1976-77," *Energy Policy in the United States*. (Ed.) S. Warkov. New York: Praeger Publishers.

Mitchell, R.C. (1978), "The Public Speaks Again: A New Environmental Survey," *Resources*, *60*, 1-6.

Murray, J.R., M.J. Minor, R.F. Cotterman, and N.M. Bradburn (1974), *The Impact of the 1973-74 Oil Embargo on the American Household*. Natural Opinion Research Center: University of Chicago.

Olsen, M.E. (1978), "Public Acceptance of Energy Conservation," *Energy Policy in the United States*: *Social and Behavioral Dimensions*. New York: Praeger Publishers.

Perlman, R. and R.W., Warren (1977), *Families in Crisis*: *Impacts and Implications for Theory and Policy*. Cambridge, Mass.: Ballinger Publishing.

Stobaugh, R. and D. Yergin (November 1979), Op Ed Column, New York Times.

Thompson, D.N. (1973), *The Economics of Environmental Protection*. Cambridge, Mass.: Winthrop Publishers.

Tognacci, L.N., R.H. Weigal, M.F. Wideen, and D.T. Vernon (1972), "Environmental Quality: How Universal is Public Concern?" *Environment and Behavior*, 4, 73-86.

Warkov, S. (1979), *Solar Adopters and Near-Adopters: A Study of the HUD Solar Hot Water Grant Program*. Cambridge, Mass.: Northeast Solar Energy Center.

Warkov, S. and J.W. Meyer (1982), *Solar Diffusion and Public Incentives*. Lexington, Mass.: Lexington Books, D.C. Heath.

Riley E. Dunlap, J. Keith Grieneeks,
Milton Rokeach

8. Human Values and Pro-Environmental Behavior

Abstract[1]

It is widely assumed that personal values are related to environmentalism, and it has been hypothesized that individuals motivated by Maslow's "higher-order" values are especially likely to engage in pro-environmental behavior. This study tests this hypothesis by examining the values of a sample of recyclers. Compared to a national sample, the recyclers are found to emphasize higher-order values such as aesthetics and self-actualization, and to deemphasize lower-order values such as safety and security. While the differences are reduced somewhat when the recyclers are compared to a matched subsample with similar demographic characteristics, the basic pattern of differences remains. The potential implications of the result, particularly their support for the Maslowian perspective, are briefly discussed.

Introduction

Scholars from a variety of disciplines have argued that the "ecological crisis" facing our society stems, in large part, from the primacy of values which encourage environmental degradation and from the absence of values which foster environmental preservation. Armstrong (1972:5), for example, states that, "Man and his values are the core of the environmental crisis . . . .," and this view is widely shared (see, e.g., Miles, 1978; Harblin, 1977; Swan, 1972).

Despite the emphasis placed on the role of values in contributing to our ecological problems, there is a near absence of empirical research on this topic. Thus, while there have been hundreds of studies of *attitudes* toward environmental issues (see Dunlap and Van Liere, 1978), very few researchers have attempted to study the more fundamental dimension of *values*. For example, Dillman and Christenson (1972) represents a rare attempt to measure environmental values, while Pierce (1977) is a singular effort to examine the relationship between values in general and attitudes toward environmental issues. Furthermore, to our knowledge, none of the few dozen studies which have examined environmentally relevant *behaviors* (recycling, littering, etc.) has focused on the relationship between values and such behaviors (see Dunlap and Van Liere, 1978: Sect. IV). Yet, the latter relationship is particularly important since the solution of environmental problems typically entails changing people's behavior (Cone and Hayes, 1980).[2] The purpose of this paper is to help fill this void, by reporting the results of a small study of the relationship between human values and recycling, a popular form of "pro-environmental" behavior.

Concepts

Human Values

While "human values" have been conceptualized in numerous ways, most behavioral scientists agree that values are the standards that guide or determine attitudes and behavior (see, for example, Parsons and Shils, 1962; Smith, 1969; Williams, 1970). In this tradition Rokeach (1968; 1973) defines values as beliefs either about "desired end-states of existence" such as freedom, equality or happiness (terminal values) or about "preferred modes of conduct" such as being ambitious, honest or independent (instrumental values).[3] He adds that, "Once a value is internalized it becomes, consciously or unconsciously, a standard or criterion for guiding action (and) for developing and maintaining attitudes toward relevant objects and situations . . . ." (1968:160). Values thus differ from attitudes in that the latter represent organizations of beliefs about a specific object (e.g., a racial or ethnic group) or about an activity or situation (e.g., interacting with a member of another racial group). The consequences which follow from these definitions and the perspective which relates the two concepts--values and attitudes-- have been well summarized by Ball-Rokeach:

> 1) a person may have thousands of attitudes toward specific objects and situations, but relatively few values; 2) values occupy a more central position than attitudes because they are generalized internal standards that transcend

> specific objects or situations; 3) values determine attitudes and action, so that a change in values should lead to a change in attitudes and actions; 4) values are hierarchically organized by their relative importance to one another; and 5) a person's value system and variations in value priorities account, in large part, for variations in attitude and action (1973:737).

Rokeach and his associates (1968; 1973) have been quite successful in relating values to a wide variety of attitudes and behavior--including racial, political, and religious attitudes and behavior. It therefore seems reasonable to expect that values will also be related to attitudes and behavior concerning the physical environment. Thus, in the research reported below, we examine the issue of whether there is a significant relationship between values, as conceptualized and measured by Rokeach, and a particular type of pro-environmental behavior--recycling.

Pro-Environmental Behavior

With the emergence of environmentalism as a major social movement in the late Sixties, a great deal of attention came to be focused on the contribution of personal behaviors to environmental problems. In this context, environmentalists placed considerable emphasis on fostering behaviors which presumably had an ameliorative effect on environmental problems (Schnaiberg, 1977). One such behavior is recycling, which at the individual level involves efforts to insure that materials such as paper, glass, and metals are re-used rather than becoming solid waste or litter. Ideally, recycling not only helps alleviate the problems of litter and solid waste disposal, but also cuts down on resource consumption and energy usage as well (see Cone and Hayes, 1980: Chap. 8).

In recent years the efficacy of voluntary recycling has come to be questioned, and environmentalists have consequently begun placing more emphasis on legislation such as mandatory bottle deposits (Cummings, 1977).[4] However, in the early Seventies, when our study was conducted, recycling was widely viewed as a meaningful form of behavior on the part of those concerned with protecting environmental quality (Environmental Action Bulletin, 1974). Particularly where individuals engage in recycling without being paid for the recycled goods, as in the case of our subjects, recycling should provide a good *behavioral* indicator of "pro-environmentalism." Further, studies using such indicators complement the more common practice of employing membership in a formal environmental organization as an indicator of pro-environmentalism (see, e.g., Morrison and Dunlap, 1980, and the references therein).

Theoretical Perspective

Despite a lack of research on the values which underlie pro-environmental behavior such as recycling, it is possible to make certain inferences concerning them and the conditions under which they might be activated. Albrecht (1975:578) provides a useful suggestion when he states, "It may be that only when economic needs are met can one develop an enduring concern for the quality of the environment. Until one has reached a certain level of economic security, aesthetic values may be much less important." In short, he suggests that concern about the quality of the environment may be something of a "luxury" which only the economically secure can afford. Albrecht bases this observation on Maslow's (1970; 1971) theory of a hierarchy of needs (values) in humans. According to Maslow, we can conceive of human behavior as motivated by certain needs, ranging from "lower-order needs" such as physiological and security requirements to "higher-order needs" such as self-esteem and self-actualization.[5] Maslow argues that individuals will not be motivated by the higher-order needs or values (he uses the two interchangeably) until the lower-order needs are satisfied.[6]

Albrecht relates Maslow's theory to the observation that individuals active on behalf of environmental quality tend to be considerably above average in socioeconomic status (see Morrison and Dunlap, 1980). It is likely that upper-middle-class environmentalists will have solved problems such as hunger and security, and thus be less motivated by these lower-level needs than individuals at lower socioeconomic levels. Consequently, when compared to the general public, environmentalists should place more emphasis on values indicative of higher-order needs--i.e., self-esteem, self-actualization and aesthetics.

While the above value differences can be attributed partly to differences in life conditions between environmentalists and the general public, the behavior of environmentalists cannot be accounted for solely by their higher socioeconomic status. Obviously only a small proportion of middle- to upper-class individuals actually engage in pro-environmental behaviors, such as recycling, thus emphasizing the importance of social-psychological as well as structural determinants of these behaviors. Since socioeconomic status is clearly not the only determinant of human needs and values, we further expect to find value differences between environmentalists and non-environmentalists even after socioeconomic status has been controlled--because of differential socialization, life histories, etc. In particular, given Maslow's description of self-actualization as entailing harmony with nature (1970:154, 163, 176; 1971:333), and "aesthetics" as an ultimate value (1970:51; 1971:43-44), environmentalists should place more emphasis on values indicative of these higher-order needs (self-actualization and aesthetics) than non-environmentalists of similarly high socioeconomic status.

After describing our sample and measuring instrument we will formulate two specific research hypotheses based on the above discussion, and then present data to test them.

Methods

The Measurement of Values

As our measuring instrument, we used the Rokeach Value Survey (1967), which consists of 18 "terminal values" and 18 "instrumental values." Respondents are instructed "to arrange them in order of their importance to YOU, as guiding principles in YOUR life." Form D of the Value Survey, used in this research, employs pressure-sensitive gummed labels. For each set of values the 18 labels (which include short definitions of the values as shown in Table 1) are presented alphabetically on the right-hand side of the page; the respondents' task is merely to rearrange them in order of importance into boxes 1 to 18 printed down the left-hand side of the page. The two sets of values are shown in Table 1.

Since a considerable body of evidence concerning the reliability and validity of the Value Survey has been presented elsewhere (Rokeach, 1973; 1974) we shall not repeat it here. Suffice it to say that the Rokeach Value Survey appears to provide a reasonably valid and reliable method for measuring human values. Further, as Rokeach (1973; 1974) has noted, there is a good deal of correspondence between several values on the Value Survey and Maslow's hierarchical set of needs (values). For example, the terminal value *a sense of accomplishment* seems to constitute a good indicator of a "higher-order need" (the self-actualization need) while *a comfortable life* is a good indicator of a "lower-order need" (the safety and security need). Similarly, the two instrumental values *independent* and *obedient* also appear to be good indicators of higher- versus lower-order needs (again, self-actualization versus security).

Table 1. Value Rankings of Recyclers Compared to National Sample and to Matched Sub-sample*

Terminal Values	Recyclers (N=93)	National Sample (N=1430)	p	Matched Sub-sample (N=93)	p
A Comfortable Life (A prosperous life)	13.7(14)	10.6(13)	.001	14.0(15)	--
An Exciting Life (A stimulating, active life)	11.1(13)	15.2(18)	.001	14.5(16)	.001
A Sense of Accomplishment (Lasting contribution)	7.3(7)	9.6(11)	.05	8.4(9)	--
A World at Peace (Free of war and conflict)	8.1(10)	2.9(1)	.001	3.3(1)	.001
A World of Beauty (Beauty of nature and the arts)	10.0(12)	12.5(15)	.01	12.4(13)	.05
Equality (Brotherhood, equal opportunity for all)	8.9(11)	7.6(4)	--	7.7(6)	--
Family Security (Taking care of loved ones)	5.7(3)	4.2(2)	.01	4.6(2)	--
Freedom (Independence, free choice)	6.3(5)	5.3(3)	--	5.3(3)	--
Happiness (Contentedness)	7.9(9)	7.7(6)	--	8.1(7)	--
Inner Harmony (Freedom from inner conflict)	5.9(4)	10.1(12)	.001	8.3(8)	.01
Mature Love (Sexual and spiritual intimacy)	7.1(6)	11.9(14)	.001	8.7(11)	--
National Security (Protection from attack)	16.1(17)	9.0(8)	.001	11.6(12)	.001
Pleasure (An enjoyable, leisurely life)	14.0(15)	14.8(16)	--	15.0(17)	--
Salvation (Saved, eternal life)	17.4(18)	9.2(9)	.001	12.8(14)	.001
Self-respect (Self-esteem)	5.6(2)	7.7(5)	.01	6.6(4)	--
Social Recognition (Respect, admiration)	15.2(16)	14.9(17)	--	15.7(18)	--
True Friendship (Close companionship)	7.8(8)	9.4(10)	--	8.5(10)	--
Wisdom (A mature understanding of life)	5.6(1)	8.3(7)	.01	7.6(5)	--

Table 1. (continued)

Instrumental Values	Recyclers (N=93)	National Sample (N=1430)	p	Matched Sub-sample (N=93)	p
Ambitious (Hard-working aspiring)	11.3(15)	6.9(3)	.001	9.6(9)	--
Broadminded (Open-minded)	6.0(2)	7.5(5)	--	6.4(3)	--
Capable (Competent, effective)	9.3(9)	9.4(9)	--	9.1(7)	--
Cheerful (Lighthearted, joyful)	9.6(11)	10.4(13)	--	10.9(14)	--
Clean (Neat, tidy)	15.0(17)	9.5(10)	.001	14.5(17)	--
Courageous (Standing up for your beliefs)	8.0(7)	8.1(6)	--	8.1(5)	--
Forgiving (Willing to pardon others)	7.3(4)	7.2(4)	--	9.6(8)	--
Helpful (Working for the welfare of others)	7.9(6)	8.6(7)	--	10.3(13)	.05
Honest (Sincere, truthful)	3.0(1)	3.3(1)	--	3.0(1)	--
Imaginative (Daring, creative)	10.7(13)	15.2(18)	.001	12.7(15)	--
Independent (Self-reliant, self-sufficient)	7.4(5)	10.2(12)	.01	9.8(11)	.05
Intellectual (Intelligent, reflective)	9.3(10)	12.7(15)	.05	9.7(10)	--
Logical (Consistent, rational)	11.3(14)	13.4(17)	.001	9.9(12)	--
Loving (Affectionate, tender)	8.3(8)	8.7(8)	--	6.6(4)	--
Obedient (Dutiful, respectful)	17.1(18)	13.3(16)	.001	16.0(18)	.05
Polite (Courteous, well-mannered)	13.9(16)	11.0(14)	.001	12.7(16)	--
Responsible (Dependable, reliable)	6.6(3)	6.5(2)	--	5.6(2)	--
Self-controlled (Restrained, self-disciplined)	10.4(12)	9.6(11)	--	8.3(6)	--

*Figures shown are median rankings and, in parentheses, composite rank orders.

Samples

Our sample of recyclers was obtained from patrons of two Pacific Northwest recycling centers, neither of which maintained a staff at the center nor paid for recycled goods. In June of 1973 one of the authors spent two weekend days at one center, and one weekend day at the other, and asked individuals who deposited material (newspapers and bottles) for recycling to complete a Value Survey and supply demographic data. The subjects were simply told that the researcher was surveying community residents for a research project, and *not* that they were selected because they were recyclers. (The central location of the recycling centers in both communities made this approach plausible.) Less than 10 percent of those approached refused to participate,[7] and data were thus obtained from 94 individuals.

With the exception of one Mexican-American, all of the recyclers are Anglo-American. The Mexican-American is deleted from the analysis in order to provide an ethnically homogeneous sample. The remaining 93 recyclers include 46 males and 47 females. In line with previous studies of environmentalists (see Morrison and Dunlap, 1980; Van Liere and Dunlap, 1980), the recyclers are fairly young and very well-educated.

We also have comparable value data from an April, 1971, National Area Probability Sample of 1430 adult Americans 21 years of age and older conducted by the National Opinion Research Center (see Rokeach, 1974). The national sample completed the Value Survey along with personal interviews. As expected, the national sample differs considerably from our sample of recyclers in terms of several demographic characteristics--84 percent of the national sample compared to 100 percent of the recyclers are white, 43 percent compared to 67 percent are under age forty, 12 percent compared to 73 percent are college graduates, and 40 percent compared to 45 percent report annual incomes of $15,000 or more.[8] The two samples are nearly identical in terms of sex, however, as 48 percent of the national sample and 49 percent of the recyclers are male.

In view of the significant demographic differences between the recyclers and the national sample it is necessary to control for the possible effects of such characteristics. This is the case because variables such as education and age have been found to be related to pro-environmental attitudes and behavior (Dunlap and Van Liere, 1978; Van Liere and Dunlap, 1980) and also to responses to the Value Survey (Rokeach, 1973; 1974). Consequently, to control for the effects of these variables, we drew a sub-sample from the national sample, matching it with the sample of recyclers on the basis of sex, race, age, education and income.[9] Thus, we are able to compare the recyclers both with a representative adult sample of the general public, as well as with a sub-sample of the general public consisting of individuals with demographic characteristics similar to those of the recyclers.

Hypotheses

Given the above samples and our measuring instrument, it is now possible to state more specifically the hypotheses to be tested: First, it is hypothesized that recyclers will rank values on the Rokeach Value Survey reflecting "higher-order needs" significantly higher, and values reflecting "lower-order needs" significantly lower, than will the national sample.[10] Second, since such results may be due at least partially to demographic differences between the two groups, it is further hypothesized that similar value differences will also be found between the recyclers and the matched sub-sample (although they are expected to be less pronounced since the effects of the demographic characteristics will be controlled).[11]

Results

The relevant data are presented in Table 1, which shows the median ranking for each value and, in parentheses, its composite rank order. For instance, Table 1 shows that the terminal value, *an exciting life*, has a median ranking of 11.1 among the recyclers and 15.2 among the total national sample, and a composite ranking of 13th among the recyclers and 18th among the national sample. The table also shows that the difference between the two groups in their ranking of this value is significant at the .001 level. Significance of difference is determined separately for each value by the Median Test, a nonparametric chi square test based upon the number of persons scoring above and below the median (of the combined scores of the two groups) in each group (see Siegel, 1956:111-116; Rokeach, 1973:56-57).[12]

First we will compare the value rankings of the recyclers with those of the total national sample, presented in columns 1 and 2 respectively (with significance levels shown in column 3). It is obvious that there are considerable differences between them in both their terminal and instrumental value hierarchies. For example, the four terminal values ranked highest by the recyclers are (in rank order):

wisdom, self-respect, family security, and *inner harmony.* In contrast, the national sample rank *a world at peace, family security, freedom,* and *equality* highest. At the other end of the terminal value hierarchy, *salvation, national security, social recognition,* and *pleasure* are the values ranked lowest by the recyclers, while *an exciting life, social recognition, pleasure,* and *a world of beauty* are given lowest priority by the national sample. The low ranking of *a world of beauty*--clearly the value most indicative of concern for a good environment--lends credence to the argument that environmental quality is a relatively weak value in our society. Turning to the instrumental value hierarchies we find somewhat fewer differences between the two groups, which is not surprising since there appears to be less correspondence between Rokeach's instrumental values and Maslow's hierarchy of needs than is true of the terminal values. Thus, *honest, responsible,* and *forgiving* are ranked among the highest instrumental values by both groups. However, when we focus on the lowest-ranked instrumental values, we find considerable difference between the two groups--the recyclers give their lowest rankings to *obedient, clean, polite,* and *ambitious,* while the values ranked lowest by the national sample are *imaginative, logical, obedient,* and *intellectual.* In short, an examination of the extremes of both value hierarchies reveals rather marked differences between the value rankings of the recyclers and the national sample.

First Hypothesis

An adequate test of our first hypothesis, however, requires that we examine *all* of the values which are ranked significantly different by the recyclers and national sample. Table 1 shows numerous such differences as two-thirds (12 of 18) of the terminal values, and nearly one-half (8 of 18) of the instrumental values, are ranked significantly different by the two groups. Further, the pattern of these differences tends to strongly support our first hypothesis.

Beginning with the terminal values, we find seven ranked significantly higher by the recyclers, and all but one clearly reflect "higher-order needs." Thus, *a sense of accomplishment* and *inner harmony* appear to be self-actualization values, and *self-respect, an exciting life,* and *wisdom* either self-actualization or esteem values. Similarly, *a world of beauty*--the value most logically related to pro-environmental behavior--is an aesthetic value which Maslow (1971:43-44) terms a "meta-need" or ultimate value and places above self-actualization values. The remaining value, *mature love,* reflects Maslow's belongingness and love need and, as mentioned in an earlier footnote, is difficult to classify as either a higher- or lower-order value. The supportive pattern is continued when we focus on the five terminal values ranked significantly lower by the recyclers than the national sample: *a comfortable life, a world at peace, family security, national security,* and *salvation.* All of these are "lower-order values," as they appear to be safety or security values.[13] In fact, *a comfortable life* might be considered to be indicative of physiological needs, the lowest level in Maslow's hierarchy. In sum, the differences between the recyclers and the national sample in their rankings of the terminal values are strongly supportive of the first hypothesis. This conclusion is bolstered by the fact that many of the remaining six values which are not ranked significantly different are difficult to classify as either higher- or lower-order values--especially *happiness, pleasure,* and *true friendship.*

Similar results obtain when we turn to the instrumental values, as all four values ranked significantly higher by the recyclers recyclers--*imaginative, independent, intellectual,* and *logical*--are what Rokeach (1973:8) terms "competence" values, and characterize self-actualizers. They are therefore higher-order values. In contrast, the four values ranked significantly lower by the recyclers include *obedient* and *polite,* which appear to be the antithesis of self-actualization, and *ambitious* and *clean.* The latter are defined on the Value Survey as "hard-working, aspiring" and "neat, tidy," and thus seem to qualify as lower-order concerns in Maslow's scheme. Finally, as in the case of the terminal values, many of the instrumental values which are not ranked significantly different are rather difficult to classify as higher-order or lower-order values--e.g., *cheerful, courageous,* and *honest.* The exceptions would seem to be *broadminded, capable,* and *helpful* (which all appear to be higher-order values) and *self-controlled* (a lower-order value), and for each of these values the relative rankings--while not significantly different-- are in the expected direction.

In short, we have found considerable support for the first hypothesis. The recyclers do rank values reflecting higher-order needs significantly higher, and values reflecting lower-order needs significantly lower, than the national sample. We do not encounter a single reversal of this pattern, thus providing strong support for the hypothesis. However, it is possible that many of these value differences may be due to demographic differences between the sample of recyclers and the national sample. This possibility seems especially likely since significant differences on many

Table 2. Distributions of Recyclers and Matched Sub-sample on Values Ranked Significantly Different in Table 1 (N's*)**

	AN EXCITING LIFE			INNER HARMONY			A WORLD OF BEAUTY		
	High	Medium	Low	High	Medium	Low	High	Medium	Low
Recyclers	17	37	39	51	28	14	29	33	31
Sub-sample	9	21	63	35	43	15	16	31	46
	Gamma = +.43			Gamma = +.24			Gamma = +.31		

	NATIONAL SECURITY			A WORLD AT PEACE			SALVATION		
	High	Medium	Low	High	Medium	Low	High	Medium	Low
Recyclers	8	14	71	37	34	22	13	6	74
Sub-sample	17	40	36	62	21	10	29	17	47
	Gamma = -.59			Gamma = -.45			Gamma = -.46		

	INDEPENDENT			HELPFUL			OBEDIENT		
	High	Medium	Low	High	Medium	Low	High	Medium	Low
Recyclers	37	31	25	35	37	21	4	4	85
Sub-sample	35	30	28	18	54	21	3	17	73
	Gamma = +.06			Gamma = +.22			Gamma = -.45		

*Percentages are not used because N = 93 for both recylers and matched sub-sample.

**"High" refers to ranking of 1 to 6, "medium" to ranking of 7 to 12, and "low" to ranking of 13 to 18 on the Rokeach Value Survey.

of these same values have been found between blacks and whites, high and low educational levels, and different age groups (Rokeach, 1973; 1974). Since our sample of recyclers is white, young and better educated than the national sample, it is necessary to compare it to a matched sub-sample in an effort to control for the effects of these demographic variables. In so doing we will be testing our second hypothesis.

Second Hypothesis

The value rankings of the recyclers and the matched sub-sample can be compared by looking at the first and fourth columns of Table 1 (and the significance levels in column 5). As we expected, the value rankings of the recyclers and the matched sub-sample are more similar than those of the recyclers and the total national sample--since the confounding effects of the demographic characteristics have been controlled. In fact, we end up with about half as many significant differences: six terminal values and three instrumental values. The terminal values which are ranked significantly different include the higher-order values *an exciting life, inner harmony,* and *a world of beauty* (ranked higher by the recyclers) and the lower-order values *a world at peace, national security,* and *salvation* (ranked lower by the recyclers). Turning to the three instrumental values, we find that the higher-order *helpful* and *independent* are ranked significantly higher by the recyclers, while the lower-order value *obedient* is ranked significantly lower. In short, the nine values which significantly differentiate between the recyclers and matched sub-sample provide strong support for the second hypothesis--the five values ranked significantly higher by the recyclers are all higher-order values, while the four ranked significantly higher by the sub-sample are all lower-order values.

In an effort to clarify the degree to which the recyclers and matched sub-sample differ in their rankings of these nine values, Table 2 shows their relative distributions on each value. The three categories of "high," "medium" and "low" refer to rankings of 1 to 6, 7 to 12, and 13 to 18, respectively, on the Rokeach Value Survey. These breaking points are used because of their intuitive appeal (they represent the highest, middle and lowest thirds of the terminal and instrumental value lists), and because the large number of tied rankings makes it impossible to develop categories with nearly equal numbers of cases. Further, the latter procedure results in breaking points which vary considerably among values. Finally, the distributions show the actual number of cases, rather than percentages, since N=93 for both recyclers and the matched sub-sample.

As expected, the data in Table 2 are in agreement with those presented in Table 1. Thus, there is a positive relationship (as measured by Gamma) between recycling and the three terminal values reflecting higher-order needs (*an exciting life, inner harmony,* and *a world of beauty*) and the two instrumental values reflecting higher-order needs (*independent* and *helpful*).[14] Conversely, recycling is negatively associated with the three lower-order terminal values (*national security, a world at peace,* and *salvation*) and with *obedient,* the lower-order instrumental value. Further, the degree of relationship is often moderately strong (exceeding .4 for five values). In sum, Table 2 illustrates a substantial difference between the value rankings of the recyclers and matched sub-sample. Particularly relevant is the fact that almost twice as many recyclers as members of the sub-sample (29 versus 16) rank the crucial value, *a world of beauty,* among the upper-third of the terminal values. Thus, even after the effects of their unique demographic characteristics are taken into account by comparing them with a matched sub-sample, it is still possible to differentiate the recyclers from non-recyclers on the basis of the former's emphasis on higher-order versus lower-order values.

Summary

In short, our results provide substantial support for both hypotheses. Well over half (twenty) of the thirty-six values significantly differentiate between the recyclers and the national sample. Moreover, without exception these significant differences conform to our predictions, as the values ranked higher by the recyclers are always higher-order values, while the values they rank lower are always lower-order values. Further, it should be emphasized that one of the higher-order values ranked significantly higher by the recyclers is *a world of beauty.* This is important since this value seems so obviously relevant to pro-environmental behavior--certainly a major goal of such behavior is to protect the beauty of nature. Consequently, this value should significantly differentiate between those engaged in such behavior and the general public, which it does in the present research.

When we then control for the confounding effects of demographic characteristics by comparing the recyclers to a matched sub-sample of the general public, the number of values which significantly differentiate between them is reduced to nine, although again the relative rankings of these values are as predicted. Further, a comparison of their distributions on these values in Table 2 reveals considerable difference between the recyclers and sub-sample. And finally, it should be emphasized that for nine of the thirty-six values to significantly differentiate between the recyclers and matched sub-sample is a result which is not easily attributable to chance. As Rokeach (1973:118) has noted, when comparing rankings of the 36 values for two groups, ". . . it can be expected that about two of them will turn out by chance alone to be statistically significant beyond the .05 level." Indeed, the number of significant value differences we have found between the recyclers and sub-sample compares favorably with that found to differentiate civil rights and political activists from the general public (Rokeach, 1973).

In summary, recall that we introduced our theoretical perspective with Albrecht's (1975) observation that the predominately white, upper-middle-class composition of the "environmental movement" might be understood in terms of Maslow's hierarchy of needs. Albrecht suggested that a concern with environmental quality would only develop among individuals who had solved lower-level needs such as hunger and security (thus accounting for the virtual absence of individuals from the lower socioeconomic levels among environmentalists). The import of our results is that they provide evidence supporting the existence of the value differences *assumed* by Albrecht to distinguish environmentalists from non-environmentalists,[15] and--more tentatively--the usefulness of the Maslowian theory of human needs as motivators of behavior.

Implications

Our study was designed to investigate theoretical rather than policy issues, and therefore any attempt to draw policy implications from it must of necessity be very tentative. With this in mind it may nonetheless be worthwhile to speculate on the potential implications of our results for environmental policy.

To begin with, the fact that we found a pattern of values to be related significantly to pro-environmental behavior may be interpreted as supportive of efforts to promote such behavior via value change--e.g., through environmental education (Miles, 1978). Yet, while it is possible to induce value change in controlled, small-scale settings (e.g., classrooms), it is very difficult to do so at the societal level. In addition, many factors besides values influence behavior (e.g., the cost of, and opportunity for, engaging in a particular kind of behavior), and thus one cannot assume that planned value change will necessarily lead to the desired behavioral change (see, e.g., Heberlein, 1974; Van Liere and Dunlap, 1978).

Furthermore, our study has shown that recycling is related to a particular pattern of values, or type of *value system* (Rokeach, 1973)--namely, an emphasis on higher-order values and a deemphasis on lower-order values. Whereas the priority placed on individual values such as a world of beauty can be changed experimentally (Hollen, 1972), it is much more difficult to produce widespread change in value systems. Indeed, the relative priority given to higher-order versus lower-order values is probably determined by basically immutable factors such as one's socioeconomic status and childhood socialization. Thus, changes in value systems are likely to stem from changes in socialization experiences and economic conditions, rather than from policies designed to produce such change. This suggests that relatively uncontrollable factors such as economic conditions will undoubtedly exert a significant impact on future value change.

Recently Etzioni (1975) and Inglehart (1977) have drawn on the Maslowian perspective to offer relatively optimistic projections concerning our society's ability to cope with environmental problems and resource scarcities. First, they note that recent decades of affluence seem to have spawned increasing adoption of "post-materialist" (or higher-order) values among citizens of the Western world. Then, arguing that such values tend to lead to less materialistic and thus more environmentally benign lifestyles, they suggest that Western nations may therefore be able to adapt successfully to an era of reduced consumption necessitated by ecological constraints such as pollution and resource shortages. In fact, Etzioni (1975) stresses the importance of promoting higher-order pursuits as a means of reducing our commitment to a materialistic way of life.

Unfortunately, the era of rising affluence that likely generated the dramatic increase in post-materialism may have come to an end in the Seventies, as rampant inflation (stemming in part from the rising cost of finite fossil fuels) has reduced the standard of living for many Americans and citizens of other Western countries during the past decade.[16] Since the Maslowian perspective suggests that higher-order needs emerge only after security needs are met, we may well see less emphasis on post-materialistic values as more and more people find that they cannot take economic security for granted.[17] Thus, we again see that factors largely beyond the control of policy-makers, such as economic conditions, may exert a powerful influence on citizen values and consequent behavioral predispositions.

To end on a somewhat more positive note, we will point out a final implication of our study which may be of more use to policy-makers. To the extent that our results support the validity of the Maslowian perspective, they also yield a rather optimistic, and potentially useful, implication. At the time of our study environmental quality was seen primarily as an aesthetic issue, and thus one appealing mainly to those who could afford the luxury of pursuing higher-order values. With each passing year, however, the public has seen that pollution is not simply unaesthetic, but that it is unhealthy too! Widely publicized incidents such as Love Canal have made it clear that environmental problems threaten the health and well-being of people, not just wildlife or the "natural" environment. Likewise, gas and oil shortages have also been seen as having deleterious impacts on people, ranging from minor inconveniences to death from inadequate household heating. In other words, pollution control, resource conservation, and other pro-environmental behaviors are being seen as increasingly relevant to the well-being and security of human beings--i.e., to lower-order needs. To the extent that policy-makers can heighten this awareness, they may be able to broaden the base of public support for environmental policies (see Dunlap and Van Liere, 1977, for a similar argument).

In sum, the more that environmental issues such as pollution and resource scarcity are seen as threatening lower-order needs such as family security, the more likely they will be seen as issues which are relevant to all citizens--and not just the well-to-do who have solved the problems of feeding, housing, and caring for a family. Further, this view of environmental issues should also help maintain widespread public concern for them even during an era of declining economic conditions. It seems clear, then, that policy-makers would be wise to emphasize that pollution, resource shortages, and other evironmental problems pose direct and serious threats to the health and well-being of the public.

Notes

[1]This is a revision of a paper presented at the Annual Meeting of the Pacific Sociological Association, Victoria, British Columbia, April, 1975, and is Scientific Paper No. 4349, Agricultural Research Center, Washington State University, Pullman, Washington, 99164. The research was supported in part by Dunlap's Project 0158, Department of Rural Sociology, Washington State University, and in part by a grant from the National Science Foundation to Milton Rokeach. The authors are grateful for this support and for the helpful comments of Viktor Gecas, Allan Schnaiberg and Rex Warland on earlier drafts of the paper.

[2]It should be stressed that there are a variety of ways of producing behavioral change, in addition to inducing it via value change. Indeed, although it is possible to change behavior via experimentally induced value change (Rokeach, 1973), Heberlein (1974) has argued persuasively against the efficacy of this approach (and similar "cognitive" strategies) for changing environmental behaviors on a widespread basis. In fact, numerous writers have suggested that a "behavioral" strategy (which rewards pro-environmental behaviors and penalizes anti-environmental behaviors) or a "structural" strategy (which removes opportunities to engage in anti-environmental behavior) are likely to be more efficacious than the cognitive strategy (see, e.g., Dunlap, 1981; Heberlein, 1974; Olsen, 1977). Nonetheless, because the cognitive approach (which attempts to produce behavioral change *voluntarily* via campaigns to alter attitudes, beliefs, or values) is the most politically feasible and popular strategy, it is important to develop a better understanding of the relationship between values and environmental behaviors.

[3]Rokeach (1973:12) regards terminal and instrumental values as ". . . two separate yet functionally interconnected systems, wherein all the values concerning modes of behavior are instrumental to the attainment of all the values concerning end-states."

[4]This shift in tactics reflects, in part, a shift away from reliance on a cognitive strategy, which employs information campaigns to stimulate voluntary participation in recycling, to the behavioral and structural strategies outlined in the first footnote. For example, a mandatory bottle deposit law aims at stimulating recycling via economic incentives, and thus represents the behavioral approach, while a law *banning* non-returnable containers as well as requiring deposits on returnables combines the behavioral and struc-

tural approaches--in that consumers are not given the opportunity to buy beverages in non-returnable containers.

[5]Maslow's (1970: Chap. 4) five-step hierarchy consists of "physiological," "safety," "belongingness and love," "esteem," and "self-actualization" needs. Since it is difficult to classify belongingness and love as either a "higher-order" or "lower-order" need we will not attempt to do so, and will use "lower-order" to refer to physiological and safety needs, and "higher-order" to refer to esteem and self-actualization needs. In his later work Maslow (1971:133-135) adds "meta-needs" or ultimate values (e.g., truth and beauty) to his original hierarchy, placing them---somewhat ambiguously--above self-actualization needs.

[6]We recognize that the concept of "need" is not popular in the social sciences. However, it should be emphasized that Maslow uses the concept in a useful and theoretically meaningful manner. Further, as Etzioni (1968) argues, judicious use of "human needs" seems warranted and can help correct the "over-socialized man" notion prevalent in modern sociology. Finally, the emphasis in this paper is on values as the cognitive or symbolic representation of needs, and as Rokeach (1973:20) notes, "Values are the cognitive representation not only of individual needs but also of societal and institutional demands." Thus, reliance on Maslow's hierarchy of needs is simply a way of helping us gain a better understanding of human values and their influence on behavior. For a similar perspective, see Inglehart (1977).

[7]An effort was made to approach every individual who deposited goods for recycling, and this was generally accomplished. The exceptions were when two or three recyclers arrived almost simultaneously. In these instances the researcher contacted the first to arrive, and the later arrivals sometimes left before he could approach them.

[8]The fact that the two samples differ greatly on education, but only slightly on income, is due in part to age differences. The generally younger recyclers were more likely to be in college or the early stages of a career. In addition, studies of members of environmental organizations have found them to differ from the general public more in terms of high educational levels than high incomes (Morrison and Dunlap, 1980).

[9]We were able to pair 75 of the recyclers with members of the national sample who shared all five demographic characteristics. Of the remaining 18 pairs created, 8 are

mismatched on income, 6 are mismatched on sex, 1 is mismatched on age, and 3 are mismatched on both sex and income. The following categories were used in matching: age--20-29, 30-39, 40-49, 50-59, 60+; education--some high school, high school graduate, some college, college graduate; income--under $2,000, 2,000-5,999, 6,000-9,999, 10,000-14,999, 15,000 and over. The categories for sex are obvious, and of course all pairs are Caucasian. Finally, we should note that while we were unable to control for region via matching, we do not regard this as a critical shortcoming. First, a national survey conducted in 1971 (the same year the value data were gathered in the NORC survey) found little regional variation in environmental concern among the public. The percentages indicating "deep concern" over environmental problems were distributed as follows: East (55%), Midwest (50%), South (53%), and West (58%)--see Gallup Organization (1972:13). Second, despite the Pacific Northwest's reputation for staunch environmentalism, in reality it is primarily the state of Oregon which manifests an unusually high degree of environmentalism (see Dunlap, et al., 1979)--and our sample of recyclers was drawn from the states of Washington and Idaho. In short, we do not believe that our sample of recyclers and the matched sub-sample differ significantly in terms of the former representing a particularly "pro-environment" region.

[10]Our use of a lower- versus higher-order dichotomy is similar to Inglehart's (1977: Chap. 2) strategy of examining "materialist" versus "post-materialist" values from a Maslowian perspective, although he classifies "belonging" needs (ambiguously in our view) as a post-materialist or higher-order value wheres we see them as intermediate between higher- and lower-order values (see earlier footnote).

[11]We should note that it is possible that some members of the national sample and the matched sub-sample are recyclers. However, the effect of these samples including recyclers should be to *attenuate* the hypothesized value differences between them and our sample of recyclers. Similarly, the most plausible effect (if any) of the two-year lapse (April, 1971 to June, 1973) between the NORC survey and our recycling study would appear to be an *attenuation* of the hypothesized value differences. This is because the economy was beginning to decline in 1973, and thus one would expect to have found slightly more emphasis being placed on lower-order needs among the public at that time than in 1971 when the NORC survey was conducted.

[12]We realize the Median Test assumes that median scores are statistically independent, whereas *ranking* in-

struments such as the *Value Survey* yield ipsative (i.e., non-independent) scores which violate the assumption of complete independence (Rokeach, 1973:42-43). However, the degree of ipsativity varies inversely with the number of items ranked, and Rokeach (1973:43) notes that, "With 18 values, the extent to which this independence assumption is violated is relatively small, the average intercorrelation (between value scores) being only -.06." In view of this small amount of non-independence, we believe use of the Median Test is justified.

[13]Some readers may prefer to think of "a world at peace" as a higher-order value, since it is a rather lofty goal. While regarding it as such has intuitive appeal, our decision to the contrary stems from a belief that the value reflects a need for "safety" and "security." This is but one instance of the difficulty of operationalizing Maslow's need hierarchy in a valid and reliable manner.

[14]The fact that the relationship for *Independent* is quite low, despite the significant difference in its median ranking reported in Table 1, is partially due to our use of only three categories. The recyclers ranking it "high" are more likely to rank it 1st, 2nd, or 3rd, while the members of the sub-sample ranking it "high" are more likely to rank it 4th, 5th, or 6th. A similar pattern occurs within the "low" category.

[15]At this point we should note that in studying recyclers we have been focusing on what Schnaiberg (1977:469) terms "meliorists"--a fairly moderate segment of the environmental movement. Had we studied more radical or committed members of the movement, we might have found even more significant value differences. This points to the fact that more research along these lines is needed.

[16]For a brief but heavily documented explication of the argument that the age of affluence experienced by the Western World (since the discovery of the "New World" and its abundant resources four centuries ago) has come to an end, and that we have entered a "post-exuberant" era, see Catton and Dunlap (1980).

[17]Inglehart (1977:383-385) believes that post-materialist values will survive a decline in the standard of living, at least in the short-run, because the values are the product of experiences during childhood and youth, and are unlikely to be altered significantly by subsequent experiences.

References

Albrecht, S.L. (1975), "The Environment as a Social Problem," *Social Problems as Social Movements.* A.L. Mauss (ed.). Philadelphia: J.B. Lippincott.

Armstrong, T.R. (ed.) (1972), *Why Do We Still Have An Ecological Crisis?* Englewood Cliffs, N.J.: Spectrum Books.

Ball-Rokeach, S.J. (1973), "Values and Violence: A Test of the Subculture of Violence Thesis," *American Sociological Review 38,* 736-749.

Catton, W.R., Jr. and R.E. Dunlap (1980), "A New Ecological Paradigm for Post-Exuberant Sociology," *American Behavioral Scientist 24,* 15-47.

Cone, J.D. and S.C. Hayes (1980), *Environmental Problems/Behavioral Solutions.* Monterey, Calif.: Brooks/Cole.

Cummings, L.D. (1977), "Voluntary Strategies in the Environmental Movement: Recycling as Cooptation," *Journal of Voluntary Action Research 6,* 153-160.

Dillman, D.A. and J.A. Christenson (1972), "The Public Value for Pollution Control," *Social Behavior, Natural Resources, and the Environment.* W.R. Burch, Jr., N.H. Creek, Jr. and L. Taylor, (eds.). New York: Harper & Row.

Dunlap, R.E. (1981), "Promoting Collective Action for Human Survival," *Adaptation, Environment and Population-Megacrisis Resolution.* J.B. Calhoun, (ed.). New York: Praeger. In press.

Dunlap, R.E. and K.D. Van Liere (1977), "Land Ethic or Golden Rule," *Journal of Social issues 33,* 200-207.

Dunlap, R.E. and K.D. Van Liere (1978), "Environmental Concern: A Bibliography of Empirical Studies and Brief Appraisal of the Literature." Public Administration Series Bibliography P-44. Monticello, Ill.: Vance Bibliographies.

Dunlap, R.E., K.D. Van Liere and D.A. Dillman (1979), "Evidence of Decline in Public Concern with Environmental Quality," *Rural Sociology 44,* 204-212.

Environment Action Bulletin (1974), "Special Issue: Recycling." EAB 5 (January), 1-8.

Etzioni, A. (1968), "Basic Human Needs, Alienation and Inauthenticity," *American Sociological Review 33,* 870-885.

Etzioni, A. (1975), "A Creative Adaptation to a World of Rising Shortages." *ANNALS, AAPSS 420,* 98-110.

Gallup Organization, Inc. (1972), "The U.S. Public Considers its Environment: Survey II," Princeton, N.J.: The Gallup Organization, Inc.

Harblin, T.D. (1977), "Mine or Garden? Values and the Environment--Probable Sources of Change in the Next Hundred Years," *Zygon 12,* 134-150.

Heberlein, T.A. (1974), "The Three Fixes: Technological, Cognitive, and Structural." *Water and Community Development: Social and Economic Perspectives.* D.R. Field, J.C. Barron and B.F. Long, (eds.). Ann Arbor, Mich.: Ann Arbor Science Publishers.

Hollen, C.C. (1972), *Value Change, Perceived Instrumentality, and Attitude Change.* Unpublished Doctoral Dissertation, Michigan State Univ.

Inglehart, R. (1977), *The Silent Revolution: Changing Values and Political Styles Among Western Publics.* Princeton, N.J.: Princeton University Press.

Maslow, A.H. (1970), *Motivation and Personality, 2nd. Ed.* New York: Harper & Row.

Maslow, A.H. (1971), *The Farther Reaches of Human Nature.* New York: Viking Press.

Miles, J.C. (1978), "The Study of Values in Environmental Education," *Journal of Environmental Education 9,* 5-17.

Morrison, D.E. and R.E. Dunlap (1980), "Elitism, Equity, and Environmentalism," Paper presented at the Annual Meeting of the American Sociological Association, New York.

Olsen, M.E. (1978), "Public Acceptance of Energy Conservation," *Energy Policy in the United States: Social and Behavioral Dimensions.* S. Warkov, (ed.). New York: Praeger.

Parsons, T. and E. Shils (1962), "Systems of Value-Orientation," *Toward a General Theory of Action*. T. Parsons and E. Shils, (eds.). New York: Harper & Row.

Pierce, J.C. (1979), "Water Resource Preservation: Personal Values and Public Support," *Environment and Behavior 11*, 147-161.

Rokeach, M. (1967), *Value Survey*. Sunnyvale, Calif.: Halgren Tests.

Rokeach, M. (1968), *Beliefs, Attitudes, and Values: A Theory of Organization and Change*. San Francisco: Jossey-Bass.

Rokeach, M. (1973), *The Nature of Human Values*. New York: Free Press.

Rokeach, M. (1974), "Change and Stability in American Value Systems, 1968-1971," *Public Opinion Quarterly 38*, 222-238.

Schnaiberg, A. (1977), "Politics, Participation, and Pollution: The Environmental Movement," *Cities in Change: A Reader in Urban Sociology, 2nd. ed*. J. Walton and D. Carns, (eds.). Boston: Allyn and Bacon.

Siegel, S. (1956), *Nonparametric Statistics for the Behavioral Sciences*. New York: McGraw-Hill.

Smith, M.B. (1969), *Social Psychology and Human Values*. Chicago: Aldine.

Swan, J.A. (1972), "Attitudes and Values in Environmental Education," *Why Do We Still Have an Ecological Crisis?* T.R. Armstrong, (ed.). Englewood Cliffs, N.J.: Prentice-Hall.

Van Liere, K.D. and R.E. Dunlap (1978), "Moral Norms and Environmental Behavior: An Application of Schwartz's Norm-Activation Model to Yard Burning," *Journal of Applied Social Psychology 8*, 174-188.

Van Liere, K.D. and R.E. Dunlap (1980), "The Social Bases of Environmental Concern: A Review of Hypotheses, Explanations and Empirical Evidence," *Public Opinion Quarterly 44*, 181-199.

Williams, R. (1970), *American Society: A Sociological Interpretation, 3rd Ed*. New York: Alfred A. Knopf.

William L. Rankin

9. The Influence of Human Values on Conservation and Energy Shortage Beliefs

Abstract

While technical facts have often been brought to bear, more wide-ranging issues such as lifestyles and the need for energy independence have also entered into debates in the field of energy. This has led to the recognition that different value positions may be the reason for divergent energy beliefs and attitudes. The relationship between human values, as defined by Rokeach, and energy beliefs and attitudes is examined using the results of a four-wave mail-out survey conducted in Washington in 1977. It is concluded that underlying value patterns are only slightly related to beliefs about future energy shorages. However, human values are more strongly related to beliefs about conservation and are most strongly related to beliefs and attitudes about specific energy technologies. Values regarding a comfortable life, national security, family security, and a world of beauty seem to be most important in this regard.

Introduction

Debates in the field of energy have become more numerous and vociferous in the past decade, largely as a result of the growth of the environmental movement. While technical facts are often brought to bear, more wide-ranging issues such as lifestyles and the need for energy independence have also entered the debate. This has lead to the recognition that different value positions may be the reason for divergent beliefs and attitudes about such issues as the likelihood of energy shortages, the efficacy of conservation, and the acceptabililty of different energy-producing technologies, especially nuclear power. In line with this recognition, the National Environmental Policy Act

(1969) asks that presently unquantified environmental amenities and values be considered in making decisions that could significantly affect the environment, along with economic and technical factors. On the face of it, this seems to be a challenging, but perhaps puzzling, task -- to use presently unquantified values in decision-making. In this chapter I would like to consider what these unquantifiable values are, how they influence energy-related beliefs and attitudes, and how they might be used in the environmental decision-making process.

Unfortunately, in much of the past research on environmental values there has been a lack of clear definition and, hence, measurement of the value concept. Consider three recent publications that purported to discuss the relationship of values to energy technology concerns: Maynard, Nealey, Hebert, and Lindell's (1976) *Public Values Associated with Nuclear Waste Disposal*, Tribe, Schelling, and Voss' (1976) edited book *When Values Conflict*, and Sayre's (1977) edited book *Values in the Electric Power Industry*. None of these publications, despite the titles, give any clear indication as to the meaning of the value concept. In the Maynard et al. (1976) report, values are the importance ratings that subjects give to four attributes of a nuclear waste management system. In the Tribe et al. (1976) book, environmental values are often equated with the (monetary) value that individuals place on a given environmental system. To her credit, one of the authors of the Sayre (1977) edited book, Maher (1977), defined values as "preferences represented in judgments that objects or states of affairs are good or bad . . ." (p. 150), although good/bad judgments about objects are usually considered to be indicators of an attitude (see Chapter 1) and the states of affairs included such concepts as optimism and faith in technology. In addition, there are those, such as Fischhoff, Slovic, and Lichtenstein (in their chapter of this book), who believe that values are hard to measure and those, such as Handy (1970), who believe that values cannot be measured.

Fortunately, Milton Rokeach (1968; 1973) believed that a long history of the value concept in the psychological, sociological, and anthropoligical literatures had led to enough clarification so that values could be operationalized and measured. Since the Rokeach value concept has been clearly defined and discussed in this book (see Chapter 8), further clarification will not be provided here. What will be presented and discussed are: value system differences among the general public, environmentalists, and a generally pro-energy population living near the Hanford Reservation; the influence that human values have on beliefs about energy shortages, the efficacy of conservation to forego future energy shortages, the relationship of electricity to the economy, and nuclear and nonnuclear energy technologies; and a different way of gaining an understanding into value/energy belief relationships that is more easily understood by nonscientists. These results are taken from a survey conducted in the state of Washington in the fall of 1977.[1]

Survey Design and Final Samples

A four-wave mail-out survey technique (Dillman, 1978) was used to gather value, belief, and attitudinal data in the fall of 1977 from Washington residents, nuclear neighbors, and environmentalists. The random sample of Washington residents was selected from a state-wide household directory. Of the 1,350 mail-outs, 96 were not deliverable and 600 were returned, yielding a final response rate of 48 percent. Women, the young, and the low socioeconomic status respondents were slightly under-represented in the final sample. In addition to the general public sample, two special samples were drawn. First, an additional random sample of 150 "nuclear neighbors" was drawn from the Tri-Cities area next to the Hanford Reservation in central Washington. Of these 150 mail-outs, 11 were not deliverable and 71 were returned for a 51 percent response rate. This sample is presented here because it not only represents a fairly strong pronuclear population, but also because the sample is proenergy and progrowth more generally. Second, a 100-person sample was randomly drawn from the mailing list of an environmental group in the state of Washington. Of these 100 mail-outs, 10 were not deliverable and 57 were returned for a response rate of 63 percent. This sample is presented because it represents an ongoing social movement whose purpose is to influence environmental decisions. The end-state value portion of the Value Survey (Rokeach, 1967) was used, and belief and attitudinal data were collected using five-point rating scales. While a major portion of the survey dealt with nuclear power, items regarding energy shortages, conservation, and other energy alternatives were also included.[2]

Results and Discussion

In this section, the values of the three groups will first be discussed. The relationship of human values to beliefs about energy shortages, conservation, electricity and the economy, solar power, and nuclear power will follow. The discussion on nuclear power will include results from an additional method for examining value/energy belief relationships.

Table 1. Average Ranking of Terminal Values for Washington Residents, Nuclear Neighbors, and Environmentalists.

Terminal Values	Washington* Residents	Nuclear* Neighbors	Environ- mentalists	p
A comfortable life	10.6(13)	10.3(12.5)	14.6(16.5)	.01
An exciting life	12.3(16)	12.8(16)	10.9(13)	
A sense of accomplishment	8.9(8)	8.2(6)	9.7(11.5)	
A world at peace	6.3(3)	6.3(3)	4.5(1)	.05
A world of beauty	11.3(15)	11.8(15)	7.0(6)	.01
Equality	9.8(11)	10.2(11)	7.5(8)	.01
Family security	5.3(1)	4.7(1)	6.8(5)	.01
Freedom	5.6(2)	5.8(2)	6.2(3)	
Happiness	8.1(6)	8.7(8)	9.7(11.5)	.05
Inner harmony	8.8(7)	9.2(9)	7.3(7)	.05
Mature love	10.4(12)	11.5(14)	9.1(10)	.05
National security	9.5(9)	7.6(5)	13.0(14)	.01
Pleasure	13.7(17)	14.4(17)	14.2(15)	
Salvation	10.8(14)	10.3(12.5)	15.1(18)	.01
Self-respect	7.7(5)	8.3(7)	6.6(4)	
Social recognition	14.8(18)	14.5(18)	14.6(16.5)	
True friendship	9.6(10)	9.6(10)	8.4(9)	
Wisdom	7.5(4)	6.9(4)	5.6(2)	.05

*Composite rank orderings are given in parentheses.

Value System Differences

The end-state value systems for the general Washington sample, the nuclear neighbors, and the environmentalists are presented in Table 1. One-way analyses of variance (ANOVAs) were conducted to determine whether the three groups differed significantly ($p < .05$) on the importance placed on the end-state values.[3] The importance placed on 11 of the 18 values differed significantly among the groups. These values were a comfortable life, a world at peace, a world of beauty, equality, family security, happiness, inner harmony, mature love, national security, salvation, and wisdom. For all the values save one (national security), the Washington residents and the nuclear neighbors placed the same importance on the values, while both groups differed significantly from the environmental group on all 11 values. Compared to the other two samples, environmentalists placed more importance on a world at peace, a world of beauty, equality, inner harmony, mature love, and wisdom and placed less importance on a comfortable life, family security, happiness, national security, and salvation. Regarding national security, the nuclear neighbors placed significantly more importance on this value than did the Washington residents, who, in turn, placed significantly more importance on this value than did the environmentalists.

These findings are much the same as those presented by Dunlap et al. in Chapter 8, except for two major differences. First, environmentalists in this study placed significantly more importance on equality than did the other two groups. Dunlap et al. did not find this difference, but should have predicted it using their theory. Second, while Dunlap et al. found that recyclers placed less importance than national sample respondents on a world at peace, this study found just the opposite -- i.e., environmentalists placed more importance than the general Washington residents and the nuclear neighbors on a world at peace. Dunlap et al. argued that their finding is consistent with a world at peace being a "lower order, safety-related" value. However, it could be argued that individuals do not concern themselves with such an abstract concept as world peace, especially during peace time, unless basic personal and familial security needs have been met. Thus, because of their generally higher socioeconomic status, a world at peace should be more important to environmentalists compared with others. Regardless, it is clear that a major concern that environmental groups have about nuclear power has had to do with nuclear weapons proliferation, which has a direct relationship to a world at peace. However, as

Dunlap et al. suggested, these value differences may be due to differences in socioeconomic status as opposed to "environmentalism." They tried to disentangle this problem through the selection of a control group matched on economic status. A different approach for controlling the effects of other variables in significance testing is analysis of covariance (ANCOVA). ANCOVA is a statistical technique that allows one to adjust each respondent's score on dependent measures on the basis of how much other variables (covariates) affect those measures. Since respondent sex, age, education, and income have been shown to be related to energy-related beliefs and attitudes (Melber, Nealey, Hammersla, and Rankin, 1977), these four variables were used as covariates, and the three samples were compared for significant differences on their value importance rankings using ANCOVA.

These results differed a little from Dunlap et al. Using their specially selected control group, they found that the recyclers and nonrecyclers differed on six terminal values, including an exciting life, inner harmony, a world of beauty, a world at peace, national security, and salvation. The ANCOVA found that the groups differed significantly [$F\ (2,621) \geq 2.99$, $p < .05$] on seven values: a comfortable life, a world at peace, a world of beauty, equality, family security, national security, and salvation. As with ANOVA findings, the general sample and the nuclear neighbors did not suffer significantly on the values (except, again, on national security), but differed significantly with the environmental group. Thus, unlike Dunlap et al., no differences were found on an exciting life and inner harmony, while the groups did differ on a comfortable life, equality, and family security. And, again, a world at peace was most important to the environmentalists compared to the other two groups in this analysis, while Dunlap et al. found that recyclers placed less importance on a world at peace compared to their nonrecycler samples. These differences may be due to differences in the samples. While this study's analysis is done on data collected simultaneously on three samples of respondents from the same state, Dunlap et al. compared a nonrandom 1973 sample of recyclers from two cities in the Pacific Northwest to a 1971 random sample of the American public over age 18, and to a subsample of this public chosen on the basis of socioeconomic status. In particular, the changing status of the Vietnam War from 1971 to 1973 may account for the reason why Dunlap et al. found less importance placed on a world at peace by the 1973 recycler sample.

It is also important to note the differences between the ANOVA and ANCOVA findings. First, except for salvation, the seven values that still differ significantly by ANCOVA seem to be related to environmental concerns. Second, the values that are no longer significantly different among groups -- happiness, inner harmony, mature love, and wisdom -- seem less related to environmental concerns. These two points are supported by the data on nuclear power that are presented at the end of this section. These findings suggest that at least six of the terminal values could be considered "environmental" values. In summary, the members of the environmental group have value systems that differed greatly from the value systems of the general Washington public and of the nuclear neighbors, even when socioeconomic status was taken into consideration. While these findings suggest that values play a role in determining energy-related beliefs, the following results come from a more direct way of analyzing these relationships.

Predicting Energy Beliefs with Values

Several items regarding energy shortages were used in the survey. Respondents were asked to indicate whether they strongly agreed (-2), agreed (-1), neither agreed nor disagreed (0), disagreed (+1), or strongly disagreed (+2) with the belief statements, "The U.S. will have a serious energy shortage within the next 10 years," and "The U.S. will have a serious energy shortage within the next 25 years." All three respondent groups slightly agreed, on the average, with both statements. In fact, the environmentalists were more of the belief that energy shortages were forthcoming than were the general public sample and the nuclear neighbors. On the 10-year shortage item, the average scores for the general public, nuclear neighbors, and environmentalists were, respectively, -0.33, -0.40, and -0.67. The average response for the general public compared to the nuclear neighbors did not differ significantly, but the environmentalists agreed with the statement more ($p < .05$) than the other two respondent groups. On the 25-year energy shortage item, the average group responses did not significantly differ. The average responses for the general public, nuclear neighbors, and environmentalists were, respectively, -0.90, -0.76, and -1.00, which means that they generally "agreed" that there will be a serious energy shortage within the next 25 years. Thus, all three groups generally believe that a serious shortage is likely, especially in the next 25 years.

Do personal value systems influence one's belief about energy shortages? This question was answered by using multiple regression (*R*) analysis to predict one's response to the belief item using the value importance rankings. In this analysis, and in subsequent regression analyses, a stepwise multiple regression approach was used, whereby values were allowed to enter the regression equation in order of their ability to predict one's belief or attitude. Only values that had significant weights ($p < .05$) were allowed to enter the regression equation. In addition, only the general population sample was used in the regression analysis.

Given that the environmentalists, the nuclear neighbors, and the general sample, despite value system differences, differed very little in their beliefs about energy shortages, it is not surprising that personal values did not seem to influence energy shortage beliefs among members of the general public. None of the values were significant predictors of one's belief about the 25-year energy shortage. With regard to one's 10-year energy shortage belief, one value, a comfortable life, entered the stepwise regression equation. However, the measure of association was quite small ($R = .10$) as was the explained variance ($R^2 = .01$). Thus, human values seem to have very little influence on one's belief about upcoming energy shortages.

Given that respondents, in general, believed in upcoming energy shortages, it is important to ask what kind of an effect they believe it will have on the economy. While not asked directly in this manner, respondents were asked to agree or disagree with the statement, "If the U.S. does not increase the production of electricity, the U.S. economy will decline." All three samples differed significantly on their average response to this question. The nuclear neighbors agreed with the statement (-1.00) and the general Washington public agreed, but to a lesser degree (-0.57). However, the environmentalists disagreed with the statement (+0.65).

Given these large belief differences, it is not surprising that values predict one's electricity/economy belief better than values predict one's energy shortage belief. Five values entered the prediction equation before the significance criterion was not met. They entered in the following order: national security, equality, a world of beauty, a comfortable life, and a sense of accomplishment. The measure of association was much larger ($R = .28$) as was the explained variance ($R^2 = .08$). Thus, values seem to play a more important role in helping to determine one's belief about the relationship between electricity production and the economy.

Given that, in general, people believe that a serious energy shortage is imminent, it is important to determine one's beliefs about different ways of coping with the shortage. The two main methods of coping with an upcoming energy crisis are energy conservation (cutting back use and/or increasing efficiency) and increased energy production. Since almost everybody is in favor of conservation, asking about one's attitude to conservation, respondents were asked to agree or disagree with the belief statement, "Paying more attention to conservation would make increased electrical power production unnecessary." The three respondent groups differed significantly from each other in their average response to this item. The nuclear neighbors disagreed (+0.84) with the statement and the general public sample disagreed slightly (+0.22), while the environmentalists agreed (-0.78) with the statement.

Again, values seemed to play some role in determining this belief. Four values entered the stepwise multiple regression analysis run on the general sample: equality, freedom, a comfortable life, and a world at peace. The measure of association (R = 0.27) and the explained variance (R = 0.07) were about the same as for the electricity/economy belief item.

There are presently two major lines of thought regarding increased energy production. They have to do with selecting between the so-called "soft energy" path and the "hard energy" path. The soft path includes increased energy conservation and the use of so-called renewable energy resources, including solar power, which is seen as the best hope for near-term energy production. The hard path is characterized by nuclear fission technology, nuclear fusion technology, and other highly technical, highly centralized energy production technologies. A belief item regarding solar power and an attitude item regarding nuclear power were included in the survey.

A belief item was used with regard to solar electrical production because, like energy conservation, most people think that it is a good thing and that we ought to be using or researching its potential. The item read, "Within the next 20 years, solar power will provide a large share of electrical power in the U.S."[4] The three respondent groups had significantly different average responses on this item, although the differences were not nearly as great as for the electricity/economy and the conservation belief items. The environmentalist group average response (-0.05) did not differ significantly from 0.0 ("neither agree nor disagree"), while the general sample agreed very slightly with the statement (-0.18) and the nuclear neighbors disagreed very slightly with the belief statement (+0.34).

Given this small, but statistically significant, difference, it is not surprising that only two values, a comfortable life and a world at peace, entered the regression equation as significant predictors of responses to the solar belief item. The measure of association (R = .18) and explained variance (R^2 = .03), while significant, were smaller than for the economy/electricity and conservation belief items.

The final item to be discussed here is a nuclear power attitude item. While the previous items have been belief items, and while numerous belief items were used in the survey, the attitude item data will be presented here. The attitude item has been chosen because nuclear power has received enough media attention that most people have formed some general attitude toward nuclear power, and the attitudes of the public are quite divergent. The item read, "The U.S. should continue to build nuclear power plants." The three sampled groups differed quite significantly in their average response to this item. The nuclear neighbors agreed (-1.11) that more nuclear power plants should be built, while the environmentalists disagreed (1.19) to a like degree. The general Washington public took a more neutral position, although the sample was pronuclear (-0.37).

Five values entered the stepwise regression procedure before the significance criterion was not met (in order of entry): a comfortable life, national security, a world of beauty, equality, and pleasue. The measure of association (R = .34) and explained variance (R^2 = 0.12) were larger than for any of the belief items discussed earlier. Thus, values seem to play a more important role in forming attitudes about nuclear power than they do in forming beliefs about other energy issues. Perhaps this is part of the reason why the main social debate regarding energy at this time has to do with the continued use of nuclear power.

Nuclear Power and Value Instrumentality

Because of the desire to study more closely the human value/nuclear power relationships, a second method of studying these relationships was included in the survey. In order to determine what Rosenberg (1956) termed the "instrumental potency" of an attitude object with regard to important human values, respondents were simply asked to list those values that they believed nuclear power helped them to attain and those values that they believed nuclear power hindered them from attaining (see Tables 2 and 3). In general, nuclear power was believed to help in the attainment of a comfortable life, a world at peace, family security, freedom, national security, and pleasure. This was especially true for Washington residents and nuclear power helped in the attainment of many values, with a comfortable life and national security as the exceptions.

When asked which values nuclear power hindered the attainment of, Washington residents and nuclear neighbors mainly responded with a world at peace and a world of beauty, while family security, freedom, and national security received some mention. Relatively, Washington residents and nuclear neighbors believed that nuclear power development helped more than it hindered in the attainment of important human values.

Just the opposite was the case, however, for the environmentalists. While they believed that nuclear power helped them to attain few values, they believed that nuclear power hindered the attainment of numerous values. These included a world at peace, a world of beauty, family security, freedom, happiness, inner harmony, and national security.

What is most interesting about the perceived nuclear power/human value relationships discussed above is the opposite beliefs held by pronuclear and antinuclear individuals. Pronuclear individuals believe that nuclear power helps them or society, more generally, to attain a world at peace, family security, freedom, and national security, while antinuclear individuals believed that nuclear power hinders them from attaining these very same values. These opposing beliefs about nuclear power/value relationships may serve as the basis for the conflict over nuclear power.

Summary

Three respondent groups were analyzed: a general public sample from the state of Washington, nuclear neighbors from around the Hanford Reservation in central Washington, and environmental group members from Washington. The value systems for the general public and the nuclear neighbors did not differ, save for the higher importance placed on national security by the nuclear neighbors. On the other hand, the values of the environmentalists differed quite significantly from the other two respondent groups. Compared to these groups, the environmentalists placed

Table 2. Percentage of Respondents Who Perceived Nuclear Power as Helping in the Attainment of Specific Human Values as a Function of Nuclear Power Attitude and Selected Groups

	Washington Residents Nuclear Attitude				Selected Groups			
	Pronuclear (310)	Neutral (125)	Antinuclear (111)	p	Washington Residents (556)	Nuclear Neighbors (68)	Environmentalists (50)	p
A comfortable life	34.8	30.4	19.8	.01	30.2	33.8	8.0	.01
An exciting life	1.3	3.2	1.8		1.8	1.5	0.0	
A sense of accomplishment	3.6	3.2	1.8		3.1	4.4	0.0	
A world at peace	27.7	13.6	9.9	.01	20.1	29.4	2.0	.01
A world of beauty	5.2	3.2	1.8		3.9	10.2	0.0	.05
Equality	3.2	2.4	0.9		2.5	1.5	0.0	
Family security	21.0	12.8	4.5	.01	15.5	16.2	2.5	.05
Freedom	18.4	6.4	7.2	.01	13.1	11.8	4.0	
Happiness	2.3	0.8	0.9		1.6	5.9	0.0	.05
Inner harmony	0.3	0.8	0.9		0.5	0.0	0.0	
Mature love	0.0	0.0	0.0		0.0	0.0	0.0	
National security	45.5	24.8	30.6	.01	37.1	47.1	16.0	.01
Pleasure	9.0	14.4	9.9		10.3	7.4	4.0	
Salvation	0.0	0.8	0.0		0.2	0.0	0.0	
Self-respect	0.3	0.8	0.0		0.4	2.9	0.0	.05
Social recognition	0.3	0.0	0.9		0.4	1.5	0.0	
True friendship	0.0	0.0	0.0		0.0	1.5	0.0	.05
Wisdom	1.6	2.4	0.0		1.4	1.5	0.0	

Table 3. Percentage of Respondents Who Perceived Nuclear Power as Hindering the Attainment of Specific Human Values as a Function of Nuclear Power Attitude and Selected Groups

	Washington Residents Nuclear Attitude				Selected Groups			
	Pronuclear (310)	Neutral (125)	Antinuclear (111)	p	Washington Residents (556)	Nuclear Neighbors (68)	Environ-mentalists (50)	p
A comfortable life	1.6	0.8	4.5	.10	2.0	1.5	0.0	
An exciting life	0.0	0.0	0.9		0.2	0.0	0.0	
A sense of accomp-lishment	0.0	1.6	1.8	.07	0.7	0.0	6.0	.01
A world at peace	7.4	20.8	35.1	.01	15.8	7.4	70.0	.01
A world of beauty	7.1	16.8	40.5	.01	15.8	2.9	52.0	.01
Equality	0.7	0.8	1.8		0.9	0.0	8.0	.01
Family security	2.3	8.8	22.5	.01	7.7	2.9	34.0	.01
Freedom	2.3	4.8	13.5	.01	5.0	0.0	30.0	.01
Happiness	1.9	4.0	3.6		2.7	2.9	16.0	.01
Inner harmony	1.3	7.2	8.1	.01	4.1	4.4	12.0	.05
Mature love	1.9	0.8	0.0		1.2	1.5	0.0	
National security	4.5	8.8	10.8	.05	6.7	2.9	14.0	.06
Pleasure	0.7	5.6	4.5	.01	2.5	1.5	4.0	
Salvation	1.6	0.0	0.0		0.9	4.4	0.0	.05
Self-respect	0.3	0.0	4.5	.01	0.4	2.9	0.0	.05
Social recognition	0.6	0.0	0.0		0.4	0.0	0.0	
True friendship	0.3	0.0	0.0		0.2	0.0	0.0	
Wisdom	0.3	0.0	2.7	.05	0.7	0.0	4.0	.05

more importance on a world at peace, a world of beauty, equality, inner harmony, mature love, and wisdom, while they placed less importance on a comfortable life, family security, happiness, national security, and salvation. When the effects of sex, age, income, and education were controlled by analysis of covariance, the differences were no longer found for happiness, inner harmony, mature love, and wisdom. The remaining seven values, except for salvation, did seem to influence energy-related beliefs, when the regression analyses data and the special nuclear power data were used for confirming evidence. The data summarized below also indicate that freedom and pleasure influence energy-related beliefs.

Another way to approach the question of how human values influence energy-related beliefs and attitudes was to use multiple regression analysis to predict the beliefs and attitudes with the value importance rankings. These analyses showed that one's energy shortage beliefs seem to be little influenced by one's values. Values did not significantly predict one's 10-year energy shortage belief, and only a comfortable life entered the regression equation for predicting ones's 25-year energy shortage belief (R = 1.0). However, in general, most people believed in upcoming energy shortages, and values were a better predictor of what people's beliefs were about how the upcoming shortages should be met. Five values entered the regression equation for predicting one's belief about the relationship of electricity to the economy (R = .28); four values entered the equation for predicting one's belief about the efficacy of conservation to forego increased electrical production (R = .27); two values entered the equation for predicting one's belief about the ability of solar power to produce electricity (R = .18); and five values entered the prediction equation for one's attitude about nuclear power (R = .34). The values that entered the prediction equations most often were a comfortable life, national security, equality, and a world of beauty.

A third method of determining which values influence energy-related beliefs and attitudes was used with regard to nuclear power. Respondents were asked to list the values that nuclear power helped them to attain and the values that nuclear power hindered them from attaining. Nuclear power was generally seen as helping the attainment of a comfortable life, a world at peace, family security, freedom, national security, and pleasure, and hindering the attainment of a world at peace and a world of beauty, and, to a lesser degree, family security, freedom, and national security. Pronuclear and antinuclear respondents generally held opposing beliefs about the relationship of human values to nuclear power.

Policy Implications

Several points can be made from the preceding results that have implications for policy makers. First, environmental values can be delineated and measured, and the relationship of these values to energy-related beliefs and attitudes can be examined in several different ways. Second, the value systems of environmentalists differ greatly from the value systems of the general public and from the value systems of generally pro-energy individuals. Third, these values seem to influence some energy-related beliefs and attitudes, but not others. In general, values do not influence beliefs about upcoming energy shortages but do influence beliefs about how the shortages should be met. Fourth, the beliefs and attitudes to which values are most closely related, especially regarding nuclear power and the efficacy of conservation to forego increased electrical production, are the beliefs and attitudes that are most controversial as social issues. Finally, values do not totally explain energy-related beliefs and attitudes. While not analyzed in this study, Rankin and Nealey (1978) have shown, for example, that beliefs about nuclear power increase one's ability to predict nuclear power attitude over the predictive ability of values alone.

These findings seem to have several important implications for policy makers. One implication is that environmental values can be quantified and the relationship of these values to energy-related issues can be determined. Thus, environmental values can be considered in the decision-making process. This information could be used in a very formal, statistical manner, such as in multiattribute decision making processes, or the information could be debated and incorporated in the general political process. A second implication of these findings is that public beliefs measured early in an energy technology research program can be used as a predictor of the extent to which the technology will or will not become a public issue. Because important groups in the debates over energy and the environment hold extremely different value positions, and because values are relatively enduring and are partial determinants of some energy-related beliefs, the debates over energy will continue. Thus, from a policy maker's perspective, he or she should be aware of the value implications of policy decisions and how those implications are likely to cause or not to cause disagreement on the policy issue.

Notes

[1]See Rankin and Nealey (1978) and Nealey and Rankin (1978) with regard to the analysis and reporting of nuclear power and nuclear waste portions of the survey.

[2]See Rankin and Nealey (1978) for a full description of the survey design and sampling.

[3]Although Dunlap et al. suggested in Chapter 8 of the book that median tests be used for these comparisons, Rankin and Grube (1980) have shown that in practice analysis of variance can be used and will show comparable results. Thus, the choice between the median test and analysis of variance is up to the user. Since pairwise comparisons between respondent groups were needed in this study, analysis of variance was used for the overall significance testing.

[4]Since the questionnaire was about nuclear power, which is important because of its contribution to electricity production, the items all referred to electricity production and not general energy production.

References

Dillman, D.A. (1978), *Mail and Telephone Surveys*. New York: John Wiley and Sons.

Handy, R. (1970), *The Measurement of Values*. St. Louis: Warren H. Green, Inc.

Maher, E. (1977), "The dynamics of growth in the U.S. electric power industry," *Values in the Electric Power Industry*. (ed) K. Sayre. Notre Dame: University of Notre Dame Press.

Maynard, W.S., S.M. Nealey, J.A. Hebert, and M.K. Lindell (1976), *Public Values Associated with Nuclear Waste Disposal* (Technical Report BNWL-1977), Seattle: Battelle Human Affairs Research Centers, June.

Melber, B.D., S.M. Nealey, J. Hammersla, and W.L. Rankin (1977), *Nuclear Power and the Public: Analysis of Collected Survey Research* (Technical Report PNL-2430). Seattle: Battelle Human Affairs Research Centers, November.

National Environmental Policy Act of 1969, Sections 102(2)(A), 102(2)(B), 42 U.S. Code Sections 4332(2)(A), 4332(2)(B) (1970).

Nealey, S.M. and W.L. Rankin (1978), *Nuclear Knowledge and Nuclear Attitudes: Is Ignorance Bliss?* (Technical Report B-HARC-411-002). Seattle: Battelle Human Affairs Research Centers, October.

Rankin, W.L., and J.W. Grube (1980), "A companion of ranking and rating procedures for value system measurement," *European Journal of Social Psychology*, 115, 1-14.

Rankin, W.L., and S.M. Nealey (1978), *The Relationship of Human Values and Energy Beliefs to Nuclear Power Attitude* (Technical Report B-HARC-411-007), Seattle: Battelle Human Affairs Research Centers, November.

Rokeach, M. (1967), *Value Survey*. Sunnyvale, California: Halgren Tests.

Rokeach, M. (1968), *Beliefs, Attitudes, and Values*. San Francisco: Jossey-Bass.

Rokeach, M. (1973), *The Nature of Human Values*. New York: Free Press.

Rokeach, M. (Ed.) (1976), *Understanding Human Values*. New York: Free Press.

Rosenberg, M.J. (1956), "Cognitive structure and attitudinal affect," *Journal of Abnormal and Social Psychology*, 53, 367-372.

Tribe, L.H., C.S. Schelling and J. Voss (Eds.) (1976), *When Values Conflict*. Cambridge: Ballinger Publishing Company.

Sayre, K. (Ed.) (1977), *Values in the Electric Power Industry*. Notre Dame: University of Notre Dame Press.

Part 3

The Use of Research Results by Policymakers

Frederick W. Allen

10. Public Attitudes and Resource Conservation Policies

Abstract[1]

Public policymakers must often make do with no more than crude measurements of public attitudes on many issues. The difficulties that policymakers commonly face are well illustrated by the recent experience of a Federal interagency committee charged with studying present and proposed policies affecting the use and conservation of material resources. This chapter reviews such problems as those of defining the issues, defining the appropriate publics, studying the complexities of the issues, and obtaining empirical data. The chapter ends with a discussion on how the lack of good information on public attitudes affects decision-making.

Introduction

President Taft once noted that "A great many people are in favor of conservation no matter what it means." (Hitch, 1978)

Taft's assertion has a ring of authority, but it is potentially misleading. Public policymakers generally do not find it easy to obtain good measurements of public attitudes on many issues. Fortunately, they are often skilled at intuitively sensing and understanding public attitudes. Because of this ability and the many other factors involved in public decisionmaking, it is not always clear how the lack of firm information on public attitudes affects the decisions they make.

Previous chapters in this book have addressed the difficulties researchers commonly face in trying to measure attitudes towards energy and material resources. This chapter describes an example of the decisionmaking environment in which policymakers often find themselves and its implications. In this case the example focuses on issues and policies concerning the conservation of material resources.

The recent (1977-1979) experience of the Federal Interagency Resource Conservation Committee illustrates very well the difficulties which public policymakers face in this area. The Committee consisted of top officials from nine Federal agencies and was directed by Congress to study present and proposed Federal policies that affect the use and conservation of material resources such as metals and forest products.[2]

Specifically the Committee examined:

1. Existing Federal tax subsidies for virgin materials
2. Extraction taxes on virgin materials
3. Subsidies for resource recovery
4. Railroad freight rates favoring primary over secondary materials
5. Product regulations directed at resource conservation
6. Beverage container deposits
7. Deposits and bounties on durable and hazardous goods
8. National litter tax
9. Local user fees for municipal solid waste
10. National solid waste disposal charge.

Good data on public attitudes concerning these policies were often non-existent. However, it is not clear how this affected the recommendations the Committee made.

The Problems of Getting Good Data on Public Attitudes

The Resource Conservation Committee faced several problems in assessing public attitudes about both the general subject of resource conservation and the specific policies it addressed.

There was at the outset a definitional problem. Going back to Taft's statement, there was the problem of defining what is meant by conservation. This question is important because what people mean by resource conservation obviously has a significant impact on how they view policies designed to achieve it. Many people have defined resource conservation using terms such as "intelligent use" of resources in the "public interest," and other terms they are so vague and high-minded that no one could oppose them and they are of no use as guides to policymaking. Other definitions boil down to nothing more than one notion or another of economic efficiency in the use of resources (Kneese, 1979).

For its purposes, the Resource Conservation Committee used the term "resource conservation" to mean consuming less virgin material resources (e.g., iron, aluminum and forest products such as paper) than we otherwise would have if no policy changes were made. As the Committee noted (RCC, 1979:3),

> Conservation can occur at any or all stages in the life cycle of a material: less total extraction; more complete use of what is extracted (less processing waste); longer-lived products and multiple use of materials before disposal (more reuse, recycling or conversion into energy); and, in the case of renewable resources such as timber, more replanting and improved husbandry of the land. Consuming less of a material also means that less of it will ultimately have to be handled as waste.[3]

As the Committee further noted (RCC, 1979:5),

> Defined in this way, the term resource conservation makes no assumptions about distinctions between materials, methods, motives, values or ultimate effects on the economy or society at large. Instead, it serves as a point of departure for evaluating existing and proposed policy choices.

These assumptions and distinctions are not part of the definition of resource conservation, but they are central to a discussion of the subject.

Another aspect of this definitional problem is the distinction between resource conservation in general and specific policy measures which are intended to achieve this general goal. It is one thing to state a preference for conservation, especially if the alternative is implied to be misuse or waste. But specific policies almost always have specific effects on specific groups which may cause decisionmakers to react differently to these policies than they would to general goals. For this reason, the expressed attitudes of people on a subject such as resource conservation are often more dependent on the choice of policies and the way they are designed than on the goals the policies are intended to serve.

This distinction introduces the second problem in understanding public attitudes on a subject such as resource conservation: to whom does the term "public" refer? Nearly everyone is in a position to make some choices every day to consume or conserve material resources; but different people in different positions make a wide variety of different kinds of choices, and when it comes to attitudes about actual means by which resources can be conserved, where they sit has a great deal to do with where they stand. This pattern was made especially clear in the public hearings held by the Resource Conservation Committee and in the letters sent to the Committee by people interested in its activities.[4]

It is important to look at resource conservation from the point of view of each of these different groups or types of decisionmakers. Each responds to related but different stimuli and incentives and each affects resource use and conservation in related but different ways. It is also important to note that the choices of one group strongly affect the choices of the others and no one group can effect a major change in resource use patterns without working with the others. The Resource Conservation Committee explicitly recognized the following types of decisionmakers in its final report (RCC, 1979:1):

1. *Individuals* purchase and use an enormous array of products in many types of packaging. When they have finished using them, a small fraction is set aside for reuse or recycling; most is simply discarded as waste. Although individuals do have opportunities to change this pattern -- through selective buying, reuse, and increased recycling -- these opportunities are generally limited and there is little incentive to take advantage of them.

2. *Private companies* decide what combinations and quantities of materials will go into their products and packaging and what to do with the scrap ma-

terials left over from the manufacturing process. Relative prices and customer preferences generally dictate these choices.

3. *Local government* officials decide what to do with municipal solid waste: whether materials and energy will be recovered from it and how residents of their community will pay the bill for waste management. Local tax and land use policies are often major determinants in these choices.

4. *Federal officials* make decisions about taxes, trade policies, subsidies, and regulations which broadly affect the choices by individuals, private companies, and local government officials to produce, consume, recycle, and dispose of materials. The full range of national goals and objectives enter into these decisions, and tradeoffs must be made among conflicting objectives.

Each of these categories, in turn, while not an "interest group" in the sense that the term is usually employed, is typically comprised itself of many separate "interest groups," whose attitudes may be very different from one another.

The variety of "publics" begins to suggest the third problem in gauging public attitudes about resource conservation: the issues are often extremely complex. The Resource Conservation Committee, with a full-time professional staff of eight, several consultants and over a dozen part-time staff in the member agencies, spent over two years analyzing and debating ten specific policies and proposals. A great number of the issues considered were very technical, involving the design of fairly complicated policies and projections of their impacts. In the end, the Committee admitted that there was still a substantial amount of work that needed to be done to understand many of the policies fully.

Under these circumstances it is not surprising to find that members of the public who are not in a position to take the time to study complex issues and policies so intensely often do not have clearly considered positions on them. Often this does not prevent people from having opinions when asked, but it makes their responses more dependent on the way the issue is explained to them. A lack of awareness about the risks and ramifications of various actions also means that behavior may not be a good indication of attitudes. Many people simply do not know or think about what their actions imply for resource use or conservation.

Where the issues are very technical it also means that many of the opinions expressed most vigorously and articulately will come from small but concentrated interest groups. The Resource Conservation Committee heard from a number of specialized industry and environmental groups, who had clear opinions on how proposed policies would affect their constituents. Each of these groups represented important points of view that needed to be considered, but they were not necessarily representative of the public at large.

The final problem that public policymakers encounter is that even where polls or other attempts at measuring public attitudes might be helpful, the work frequently has not been done. Of the ten policies which the Resource Conservation Committee considered, there was only one (beverage container deposits) on which there was any real body of information on public attitudes. On the other policies, not only did good attitudinal data not exist, but it is even unlikely in several cases (such as railroad freight rates and the national solid waste disposal charge) that many members of the public had ever considered the issues at all.

The issue of beverage container deposits, which has become for many a symbol of the larger issue of resource use and conservation, has attracted a good deal of public attention, and the members of the Resource Conservation Committee had relatively good information on public attitudes towards it. The information available to the Committee was roughly as follows: A nationwide poll in 1975 found that 73 percent of those interviewed would favor a national deposit law (Federal Energy Administration, 1976). Seven states (Vermont, Oregon, Maine, Michigan, Iowa, Connecticut and Delaware) had their own deposit laws, and similar laws had been hotly debated across the country. Polls conducted in states where deposit laws had been in effect for several years showed them to be popular; 90 percent of the respondents in Oregon and 93 percent of the respondents in Vermont favored continuing the deposit system (RCC, 1978; RCC, 1979). At the same time, similar laws had been defeated in several states, both in public referenda and in the legislatures.

One additional fact about the 1975 national survey is worth noting: it was commissioned by the Federal Energy Administration, which had become interested in the energy implications of beverage container deposits. As is evident from the previous chapters, much better attitude data have been assembled on the subject of energy than on other resource conservation issues, because of the attention that has been focused on energy. Issues on environment more generally, such as air pollution and toxic wastes, have been studied a number of times and public support for cleanup has usually been found to be strong. On the other hand, conservation of material resources has not been as much of a national priority, and public attitudes towards policies in this area have not been studied as carefully. In a sense, it didn't really take any surveys to show that conservation of material resources has not been a very important public issue: the fact that the surveys have not been done is indication enough.

How Does the Lack of Data on Public Attitudes Affect Decisionmaking?

Whatever information a public policymaker may have about attitudes concerning a particular policy, there are a number of additional considerations or constraints he must keep in mind. These constraints result partly from public attitudes on many broader issues and partly from the nature of the institutions in which officials must operate. The motivations for heeding them may include the desire to do the "right" thing on the particular issue at hand, which is generally why the individual was appointed or elected in the first place, and the desire to remain in office and be effective overall. Given these considerations it is difficult to assess how the simple lack of good information on public attitudes concerning specific policies affects the decisions made on them.

Two examples are useful to illustrate the variety of considerations that policymakers must face. First, in a speech given to a conference sponsored by the Resource Conservation Committee, Simon Straus, Vice Chairman of ASARCO, Inc., listed eleven national goals or "principles of government policy" that public policymakers must keep in mind when they make resource decisions as well as many other types of decisions. His list is not "in any particular order of priority, but simply for the purpose of enumeration" (Straus, 1979:3):

1. The necessity to fight inflation.

2. Stopping the slide in the U.S. dollar by taking measures to correct adverse trade balances.

3. Conserving non-renewable resources such as the non-fuel minerals to the extent compatible with a healthy economy.

4. Increasing the recycling of resources to the maximum extent feasible.

5. Minimizing pollution of air, water, and land.

6. Protecting the health of the general public and of industrial workers.

7. Promoting maximum employment in order to reduce unemployment.

8. Improving the standard of living. This includes human values such as, for example, recreation opportunities, preserving wilderness, etc.

9. Maintaining the freedom of the individual -- safeguarding individual liberties.

10. Keeping the nation secure in a world that is troubled, militarily and politically.

11. Preserving the private enterprise system.

In the same vein, but from a slightly different angle of approach, the Resource Conservation Committee itself explicitly laid out five criteria which it used in evaluating policies affecting resource conservation (RCC, 1979:46):

1. *Free Market Principles*. As much as possible, conservation policies should not interfere with the free choice of producers, consumers, and local governments to make decisions. This criterion is consistent with the broader democratic philosophy of freedom of choice and also represents the basic belief in the United States that the private market system should be the primary mechanism for allocating society's resources . . . .

2. *The "Polluter Pays" Principle*. In simple terms, the "polluter pays" principle means that whoever is responsible for pollution should pay for preventing, controlling, or correcting the damage. Although there are exceptions to any rule, pollution costs should be neither subsidized by taxpayers in general nor borne directly by those exposed to the pollution . . . .

3. *Social and Economic Equity*. Any significant new policy will, if effective, create changes. Often such changes will be more beneficial to some groups

than to others. The short-term consequences of a conservation policy might be that specific industries, labor groups, and geographical regions of the nation would experience "windfall" gains or losses. For example, some consumer groups may find their living costs rising much more rapidly than others as a result of a policy directed at conserving the entire nation's material resources . . .

4. *Economic Efficiency*. Economic efficiency -- the situation in which society gets the most of those goods, services, and environmental benefits it desires within the constraints of existing resources and technology -- requires comparing total social benefits with total costs to ensure that society does not sacrifice more goods and services than are justified by the benefits of the policy. . . .

5. *Administrative Feasibility and Cost*. A conservation policy should not require information or data that cannot be acquired at reasonable cost. From a practical viewpoint, the total cost of administration and enforcement of any given policy for both public administrative agencies and private parties should be small compared to the benefits derived (RCC, 1979).

One of the ways in which these criteria are useful is that they each derive from a principle that is thought to be generally accepted by the public and many of them suggest ways of measuring achievement. Moreover, in the absence of information on public attitudes concerning an individual policy they provide a way of estimating what the reaction might be. However, as many, including the Resource Conservation Committee, have found, they do not always yield consistent conclusions when applied to particular policies and there is no very exact way of balancing conflicting priorities. This is where the judgment of a policymaker is needed.

The nature of government institutions further complicates the actions of policymakers. Officials must consider the support they need from other individuals and groups, both in and out of government, in order to be able to do their jobs most effectively and remain in office. Government officials are therefore often not anxious to take unnecessary risks in this area. The attitudes of these individuals and groups can thus in effect become the most relevant "public attitudes" to which the officials must respond. These considerations can encourage officials to endorse policies which they might not otherwise have supported or which would be "unpopular". This is particularly the case for agencies that have "constituencies" and individuals who must represent the people to whom they report. In the case of the Resource Conservation Committee, the members often took positions in line with their "constituencies."

Finally, the policymaker's personal agendas and attitudes obviously play an important role. Not only do they do this directly, but they also do it indirectly, by affecting the perception of the attitudes of others. The easiest attitudes for anyone to go along with are attitudes which he shares, no matter how widely shared any study may show them to be.

Against this backdrop, it is not at all clear how the lack of good data on public attitudes to specific policies affected the Resource Conservation Committee. Although various members urged it to do so, for a variety of considerations as cited above the Committee as a whole avoided taking strong stands on any potentially controversial policies. Better data on public attitudes would have been nice to have, but may not in this case have made an important difference.

Recognizing the important role that the public ought to play in public policymaking, the final act of the Committee was to publish and widely distribute its final report, *Choices for Conservation*, which contained analyses of the ten policies it studied (RCC, 1979), together with the Committee's consensus conclusions and recommendations on each. It did this in the hope of increasing public understanding of the policies. There is a very strong need for improved public understanding of issues which affect the public at large. Not only does this make it easier for public officials to know what their constituents desire, but it also makes it more likely that they will be able to deliver. And ultimately, the combination of better measurement of public attitudes and better public understanding of issues will make it possible to test President Taft's assertion that "A great many people are in favor of conservation, no matter what it means."

Notes

[1]The views expressed in this chapter are those of the author and not necessarily those of the U.S. Environmental Protection Agency, the Resource Conservation Committee, or any government body.

[2]The Resource Conservation Committee (RCC) was established under Section 8002 (j) of Public Law 94-580, the Resource Conservation and Recovery Act of 1976. The Committee included the Administrator of the Environmental Protection Agency (Chairman), the Secretaries of Commerce, Energy, Interior, Labor and Treasury, the Chairmen of the Council on Environmental Quality and the Council of Economic Advisors and a representative of the Office of Management and Budget. A full-time staff was provided by the Environmental Protection Agency.

[3]The definition of resource conservation in the Resource Conservation and Recovery Act includes many of these elements explicitly:

> "The term 'resource conservation' means reduction of the amounts of solid waste that are generated, reduction of overall resource consumption, and utilization of recovered resources . . . which are defined as material or energy recovered from solid waste." RCRA, Section 1004, (21) and (20).

[4]Complete references are found in Appendix B (RCC, 1979).

References

Federal Energy Administration (1976), *Energy and Economic Impacts of Mandatory Deposits*. Washington, D.C.

Hitch, C.J. (1978), *Resources for an Uncertain Future*. Baltimore: Johns Hopkins University Press for Resources for the Future, Inc. (Quoting Taft from *Outlook, 5-14-10*, 57).

Kneese, A.V. (1979), "Issues in Minerals Conservation," (unpublished paper presented to the Brookings Institution Conference on *Issues in the Conservation of Non-Fuel Minerals and Timber*).

Resource Conservation Committee (1978), *Committee Findings and Staff Papers on Beverage Container Deposits*. Washington, D.C.

Resource Conservation Committee (1979), *Choices for Conservation*. Washington, D.C.

Straus, S.D. (1979), "Impact of Public Policies on Non-Fuel Minerals." (unpublished paper presented to the Brookings Institution Conference on *Issues in the Conservation of Non-Fuel Minerals and Timber*).

Lynda T. Carlson

11. The Use of Energy Survey Data in the Policy Process

Abstract[1]

This chapter outlines the nature of the surveys carried out by the Energy Information Administration (EIA) since 1976 in order to collect energy consumption data in various sectors, and discusses how these data have actually been used in the development of federal policies and programs. Although recognizing the importance of attitudinal data, EIA's first priority has been to establish an organized and coherent set of basic statistics on consumption patterns. Using this basic information, the program offices and individual utilities have been able to move forward with specialized surveys, including attitudinal surveys, relating to particular programs under consideration.

Introduction

With the onset of the energy crisis in the early 1970's it became evident that there was little reliable information available on energy end use that was relevant to the policy process. Perhaps the largest gap in information related to consumption data--who used what, when, how, and for what purpose. Basically, the only information relating to energy that the federal government collected was about supply. Consumption was defined as depletion from the primary stocks of various fuels. Precious little information was available to determine who was using the energy and for what purpose. Consequently basic information was needed that would measure and explain relevant public activities and attitudes, especially as they relate to energy consumption, conservation, and change.

In early 1976, the Energy Information Administration (then the Federal Energy Administration) commissioned the

National Academy of Sciences to undertake a study to determine what the major needs for data on energy consumption were and to specify how the data could be collected and utilized in the evaluation of public policy. The NAS committee determined that data on energy consumption were needed for three purposes: to understand energy consumption both for basic scorekeeping or benchmarking and for modeling future patterns; to formulate public policies; and to assess the impact of policy on future energy consumption (National Research Council, 1976). The committee noted that limited sets of relevant data existed in some sectors of the economy, but an organized and coherent set of statistics did not exist.[2] Therefore, the Energy Information Administration began a program to design, develop and implement a series of data collections to obtain energy consumption data in the various sectors. Energy consumption data were defined as the actual consumption and expenditure information as well as data on the characteristics of the stock that was consuming the energy. Several of the NAS committee members felt that behavioral and attitudinal data were important in determining how energy was consumed and evaluating potential policies.[3] It was, however, the basic position of the Academy and the Energy Information Administration that the first order of business was to collect the basic consumption information.

The design, development and implementation of a residential energy consumption survey, residential transportation energy consumption survey, a commercial/nonresidential buildings energy consumption survey, and an industrial energy consumption survey were begun in the 1976-1979 time period. The first work to be started was in the residential sector. The residential surveys were designed to be small scale, flexible and very timely. In these yearly surveys, data were collected on the housing units, the households, the characteristics of the stock of energy-consuming appliances, and other related information. In addition, the actual consumption and expenditures data for different fuels used by the household were obtained from the specific fuel suppliers.[4] These data were linked to the actual heating and cooling degree-day data for the billing period to allow analysis of end uses for space heating and cooling. Subsamples of the housing survey then participated, on a rotating basis, in a monthly transportation panel in which consumption, expenditures, and miles travelled data were available for each vehicle in the household. Initially a diary to obtain trip-type information was designed, but resource constraints prohibited undertaking this component of the survey.

Next a survey was developed of the commercial/nonresidential buildings stock where first-time-ever data were obtained on the characteristics of the building stock (number, square footage and other energy related characteristics), conservation related activities, and actual consumption and expenditures for energy in the buildings. A preliminary survey was also designed and implemented to obtain consumption and other related characteristics for large industrial boilers.

These surveys ran the gamut from ongoing statistical series to interim surveys that met some of the data needs of users, to surveys which were terminated. In all sectors for which data have been collected, the surveys provide information not previously obtained and which have been used for a wide range of policy purposes.

How the Survey Data Have Been Used

The data on consumption and the characteristics of the housing units and the households comsuming the energy have been used as components in a broad range of policy formulations and evaluations. The initial data on the characteristics of the households related to conservation practices were published in a preliminary form in August of 1979 (National Interim Energy Consumption Survey, 1979a, Preliminary Conservation Tables), followed by a more complete report several months later.

The conservation data were published just as the direction of the Carter energy policies was being developed. The Office of Policy utilized the data to help determine the scope of the residential energy tax credits and solar credits which they would attempt to negotiate first with the Treasury Department and then with the Congress. When EIA was designing the original questionnaire and the tabulations, the bill had not yet been signed. It was unclear how many months retroactively the bill would cover. Therefore, EIA had to ask the households what conservation activities they had completed and the month in which the activity had taken place. When the bill was signed, the data were aggregated to the coverage period. The Policy Office used the data to support their position that insufficient conservation was being undertaken by households. Policy's position at that point was that households should be encouraged, through the use of financial incentives, to undertake further conservation activities. The financial incentives utilized in this case were tax credits. In turn, various runs of the data were conducted by the Joint Tax Committee to determine alternative tax scenarios.

A second use of the initial residential data involved a policy issue related to fuel oil use by households. The data were utilized to determine the extent of a perceived crisis and what policies, if any, were needed to prevent a crisis (National Interim Energy Consumption Survey, 1979b). In the summer of 1979, a number of newspaper stories predicted that shortages of fuel oil for heating of residences and businesses would occur during the winter of 1979-1980. The refineries appeared to have large stocks of gasoline but below normal stocks of fuel oil for heating. During the early part of the summer many articles began to appear on the perceived shortages. DOE decided that it was necessary to assesse the status of households using fuel oil, to determine the extent of their stock, and the types of conservation changes they had been making to use their fuel oil more efficiently. In July, the EIA was told to ascertain the inventory and activities of the households and have the data available to senior levels of DOE and the White House by early September. After a series of design discussions and rapid pretests, the EIA implemented a quick response phone survey to the fuel oil households in the Interim Residential Energy Consumption Survey. The aim of the survey was to determine if households were experiencing problems in obtaining fuel oil. The survey also collected information on the household's expenditures for fuel oil and their conservation activities. The survey involved contacting fuel oil households and dealers, respectively.

At the end of August, preliminary results from the households were provided to senior management of EIA and DOE. Final results on the combined household/fuel oil dealer surveys were reported in mid-October. The initial results indicated that fuel oil households had a larger fuel oil inventory than they had the previous year. In addition, EIA discovered a major trend among the fuel oil housholds of insulating their homes at a very high rate. More significantly, it was noted that 8 percent of all single-family homes that used fuel oil as the main heating fuel in the winter of 1978-1979 had converted to an alternative fuel by August of 1979. These data were extremely important in the emergency planning which the DOE was then undertaking to ensure that these households would not be without heating fuels. The survey data indicated that the households could make it through the early fall with the stocks they had on hand. Because of conservation activities, if the weather approximated the forty-year norm, stocks of suppliers would last substantially longer than normal due to the conversions and conservation activities that had taken place. With the results from the fuel oil dealers survey, EIA was able to substantiate and refine the information on the household stocks and consumption. These data were very important in the development of emergency procedures for a potential shortage. The information indicated to DOE that a crisis was not imminent and that the perception of fuel oil households would not have sufficient fuel was unrealistic. Interestingly, the data (which were subsequently published) on the response of fuel oil households to rapidly rising prices--i.e., conversions and very extensive conservation activities--have been used extensively by natural gas pipeline companies and others to forecast what natural gas households might do if gas prices were deregulated rapidly.

The Relationship Between Basic Survey Data and Attitudinal and Behavioral Data

There is a very close and direct relationship between the basic information collected in benchmarking surveys such as the Residential Energy Consumption Survey and various attitudinal and behavioral studies and surveys geared to specific programs or policies. Basic data on trends provide the parameters from which policymakers and program offices can then operate. For instance, the residential data indicated that sufficient conservation might not have been taking place to meet the goals established as part of energy policies of the Carter Administration. Various policy options could be contemplated by policymakers, utilizing basic information on the characteristics of the different groups that were and were not undertaking conservation (specifically as related to their consumption, expenditures, and housing characteristics). The survey work helped the program offices pinpoint what they considered to be target populations and move forward with special surveys related to the individual programs. For instance, individual utilities around the nation are working with DOE to implement the Residential Conservation Service mandated by Congress. They are using the Residential Energy Conservation Survey data to provide them with basic statistics, and are also collecting specialized data related to their individual customers or service areas on the programs they are interested in implementing. The types of attitudinal data which the utilities are collecting deal with a household's perceived needs for information on energy conservation, types of energy-saving practices they are undertaking or might consider undertaking, the factors that impact on their decisionmaking process, and their preferred sources of information, as well as awareness of specific programs offered by their utilities. This utility-specific program data will be used in conjunction and as a supplement to the national and regional data available from the Residential Energy Consumption Survey. It would be feasible for the analysts to attach all this specific programmatic data to the broad based statistical data set.

Conclusion

This chapter has indicated that residential energy consumption survey data were utilized to help design financial incentive programs to encourage residences to conserve energy. In the future, the data from the residential and the nonresidential buildings are going to be used extensively to determine how effectively the market is operating in reducing energy consumption and encouraging energy conservation. It is likely that the data will also help determine where market imperfections are occuring and suggest what might be done to improve the situation.

Notes

[1]The opinions and conclusions expressed herein are solely those of the author and should not be construed as representing the opinions or policy of any agency of the United States Government.

[2]National Research Council (1976), Chapter 1, pp. 7-18.

[3]Ibid., p. vii.

[4]For a discussion of the Survey methodology, see Appendix A, pp. 75-90 of Residential Energy Consumption Survey (1981).

References

National Research Council (1976), *Energy Consumption Measurement*: *Data Needs for Public Policy*, Washington: National Academy of Sciences. (1976).

National Interim Energy Consumption Survey (1979a), *Preliminary Conservation Tables*, 0193/P. Washington: United States Government Printing Office.

National Interim Energy Consumption Survey (1979b), *Single Family Households*: *Fuel Oil Inventories and Expenditures*, 0207/1. United States Government Printing Office.

Residential Energy Consumption Survey (1980), *Conservation*, 0207/3 Washington: United States Government Printing Office.

Residential Energy Consumption Survey (1981), 1979-1980 Consumption and Expenditures, Part I: National Data (including Conservation), 0262/1. Washingon: United States Government Printing Office.